One of the objects of Hawick Callants' Club is "The Fostering of Local Art and Literature". When the club was given the opportunity to publish the works of David Hill, we felt that this was a very worthwhile project and fully matched the criteria required.

The finished book has added another great chapter to Hawick's rich list of publications.

Hawick Callants' Club would like to thank very much the Hill Family for allowing David Hill's lifetime of works to be published in book form of his "Ain Gait".

The club are also indebted to all who assisted in the planning, development and production of the book; without their expertise and support it would have been a much more difficult task.

President Robert Charters 2011

David Hill 1911-1977

EPITAPH ON A DUNE TALENT

There's nane of us a but keeks aboot
Wi a flickerin' candle's light,
But some hae time to write and see
And some to see and write

Acknowledgement

I would like to thank Hawick Callants' Club for the opportunity to publish a volume of my late father's work. Grateful thanks to Mrs Frances Paxton, Mr Norman Turnbull and Mr Hugh Mackay for their hard work and support in this venture. I am also indebted to the School of Scottish Studies for their past advice.

This book is dedicated in memory to my late mother Mrs Robertina Scott Hill and my late sister Miss Christine Morrison Hill.

David Andrew Hill
November 2011

First Published 2011

ISBN: 978-0-9548562-3-6

Printed by Richardson & Son Printers, Hawick
www.richardsonprinters.com

"AIN GAIT"

A collection of selected verses and writings

by David Hill

INTRODUCTION

The dulling down of the literary sensibilities as the years go by, is a phenomenon not unknown – Darwin on Shakespeare is a prime case study – to medical science. It is a complaint, or misfortune, from which one is by no means inclined to claim a personal immunity. It is therefore with something akin to relief that on turning to the body of work in this present volume, one finds it just as impressive and engaging as it had seemed when first encountered, in some of the poems, thirty-six years ago.

David Hill (1911-1977), poet, playwright, short story writer, local historian and commentator, and very occasional broadcaster, grew up in the Scottish Borders town of Hawick, in the years between the two world-wide wars of the 20thC. An advertising copy-writer in the later inter-war period, he was subsequently to inherit and carry on the family business, the making of the famous Hawick balls. He served with the R.A.F. in World War 11, finding himself at various times in England, Egypt, and Italy; wars and rumours of wars form the back-drop to a number of the poems.

While David Hill is best known locally for some deeply appreciated poems – and his poetry does undoubtedly represent his very finest work – notice of his contributions to two other fields is necessary. It is with these, rather than via the poetry (widely scattered as, in the main the latter was, over locally published newspaper issues and anthologies) that he made his considerable impact on the wider literary scene. Several of his plays were given performances on the B.B.C.'s Scottish Home Service. The short story, 'Thirty-Six Hours', was included by John Lehmann in an issue of 'Penguin New Writing'; it subsequently enjoyed translation into several European languages. A number of the stories reached national audiences, courtesy of B.B.C. readings.

Some of David Hill's poems have been much anthologized locally; many others have from time to time featured in the pages of the local press. The poet has never lacked within his own Hawick and Borders community an enthusiastic and discerning readership. This makes it the more surprising, perhaps, that the present volume is the first gathering together in book form of a representative selection of his work. Including as it does unpublished as well as published poems, short stories, 'Observations' on the local scene, and in 'Chucks-mei!', an extended meditation on the Borders, it presents a picture in the round not hitherto available. The volume will undoubtedly receive a very warm welcome from David Hill's long established Hawick and Borders constituency. It is hoped, however, that it will also serve to introduce many new readers from the wider literary community, to a very fine, and perhaps beyond the Borders, a now too little known literary achievement.

In Alan Jackson's, 'A Scotch Poet Speaks', the eponymous author expresses, rather entertainingly it has to be said, some annoyance at being interrupted while busy with his translation of "my last wee poem / Into the dear auld Lallans." Possibly not altogether without foundation, it may be thought, is the charge implicit here, that in some modern Scots verse the old, newly exotic words are scattered about in an attempt to add colour to a too low-key poetic performance. In what different and contrasting territory we are, in David Hill's major Scots poem, 'The Bleach', the opening word-pictures make very clear.

> And boulevards o' blankets ruggin' and rivin'
> At the grey, grainin' ranks o' poles that leaned
> Hauf-dazed, like deef auld men, listenin.

The sharpness and freshness of the individual vision (one thinks of Pound's demanding mantra, 'Make it New') leap out on one in "boulevards", and in the remarkable images in the lines immediately following. "Hauf-dazed, like deef auld men" is very fine. "Hauf-dazed, like deef auld men, listenin" is inspired. It fixes the scene on the reader's retina, once and forever.

'The Bleach' takes us back to the poet's early childhood, and simultaneously, if paradoxically, to our own earliest days, as well. There – over there – is the Bleach, but there too, are those blue remembered hills, which, since Housman, have stood in for so many different landscapes of the mind. When the poet recalls

> Yin distant simmer's day wi' a biscuit in my hand,
> Fresh frae the lang mysterious spicy drawer
> O' the Store Van . . .

he is telling it the way it was for us, as well as for himself. Doubtless the Store Van is optional; that spicy drawer is surely not. Mysterious it was, though it may be that it is only the poet's exactly chosen words, which now allow us to see and feel again, its long forgotten particularity.

As well as being a vivid evocation of what D.H. Lawrence, thinking of a few Nottinghamshire acres, called "the country of my heart", 'The Bleach' is a reflection on the beauty and fragility of life, and the ceaseless flow of time. A "bairn hover-doverin' in The Bleach", lost in a Wordsworthian "splendour in the grass" falls into a settled sleep. The poet remembers

> . . . gentle hands
> That wakened me, and a kindliness that knew
> The hairst o' deid that simmer on The Somme
> An yet had patience to coont ower to me
> The daisies on my cheen.

He goes on to survey a darkening Green from a double perspective. Looking back down the years he knows that "Wars come / A' in their ain wersh time." He recalls the world of the child where, in a wonderfully apt comparison

> . . . Douce as a curny dumplin'
> Sat The Moat.

In a closing passage, what lies ahead in the adult world is finely adumbrated

. . . A train cam clinkin' doon,
Snakin' atween the Slitrig hills. And the dark shadows
O' the poles lay felled and lang athort The Bleach,
The green gress o' The Bleach, now gane.

Remembered here, in the falling cadences, are both the Bleach and the dead of the century's wars.

If 'The Bleach' is David Hill's outstanding work in Scots, a reading of the other Scots poems offers many rewards. The dense Hawick/Roxburghshire vernacular of 'The Jooral-I-Joo' is the vehicle for a street scene splendidly infused with that high-spirited élan which gives such energy and life to so many of them.

The jougals yowl't at the jooral-i-joo
Whaniver hei stert' tae play;
A shilpt scurryvaig hei wes
And shuttle-gobbit tae,
And he bruisslt and whewed the bullet-shells
And bang't the drum away.

Pretensic fowk gaed primpin' by,
Snirkin at sic a din,
Only the jougals hunkert roond,
Enjoyment seemed tae fin –
Or war the critters yowlin' at
The plicht their God was in?

David Hill belongs to that select company of poets for whom rhyme is a servant not a master, and the driving rhythm here never allows us to think that we know where the poem is going before the poet gets there. If one reaches rather smartly for a Scots dictionary, and 'The Roxburghshire Word-Book' one does so with a smile on one's face; the word-music of the two stanzas makes the tribute mandatory, though the poem, on second or third reading, is not without its ambiguities. It is a remarkable tour de force.

'Owre Whita' is a beautifully crafted poem in which the landscape, and the emotional landscape fuse to form a compelling picture of lives seen in a particular framework of place and time.

Lang-syne it was
Thon souchin simmer's day,
Wi' cloods that sailed
Loutin to their shaddas
Like swans, breistin the surges
O' breckan . . .

We can wonder, but only wonder, what the poet has in mind when he finishes

> . . . mebbe yon was
> A dryer 'eer. For I mind nocht
> O' this black ineluctable peat
> That drags now at my feet.

A coda reads (For Ina and Langholm – con amore, 5/8/32, 9/12/75).

A number of the 'Hawick' poems reflect that sense – nowhere more powerfully present than in the storied burgh – that, in Edmund Burke's classic formulation, a community is a compact between those who are living, those who are dead, and those who are yet to be born. One of the main charges laid upon the bard, has always been to keep well burnished the living traditions of the tribe, and to memorably hand on to the coming generations, the tales and legends which have gathered round its heroic and iconic figures. Pre-eminently iconic in Hawick are the centuries-old Hawick Common-Riding, and Hawick Rugby Football Club. Both institutions have been much celebrated over the years by gifted Hawick writers. In terms of the modern era Common-Riding, one thinks, perhaps (the choice is very extensive) of Robert Murray's splendidly accomplished, 'The Reckoning', and the fine, 'The Exile's Return', by David Hill's friend and contemporary, William Landles.

The present volume contains two rugby poems, and in 'Common-Riding Toast' (delivered in person by the poet, at a Hawick Common-Riding Dinner) a considered and thoughtful tribute to the three Common-Ridings best known to him. If T.S. Eliot's river is a strong brown god, the poet's Teviot morphs very shortly into the river of life itself seen at Common-Riding time in Hawick as "a rip-tide . . . cairryin' a' thing afore it . . . " We have already met the Moat. Here, in another of the poet's finely judged images

> . . . the auld Moat,
> That's seen hunders o Common-Ridings,
> Sits hotchin up thonder like an ancient dowager,
> Waitin for daylicht and her dancing Callants . . .

In those "dancing Callants" is that vigorous Borders life to which David Hill responded with such sympathetic enthusiasm.

You will, if the iron has not entered too far into your soul, much enjoy, 'Robbie Dye', a long adroitly humorous, and affectionate portrait of a symbolic figure who has come to sum up in his person, what Mansfield Park, and its hallowed turf, mean to the town. 'An Auld "Dye" ', dedicated "To the fervent supporters of Hawick Rugby Football Club", captures very exactly, the match-day "weather in the streets", though the poet himself, courtesy of the bus is roarin up throwe the Mansfield mirk, for hame;

chaffin and argyin; clashin oot praise and blame
. . . Yin mair, yin less; that's mortal law;
but won or lost; sunshine or blatterin weet;
how guid it's been, man, seiin them rin the ba!

The poem recalls nothing so much as the L.S. Lowry painting, 'Going to the Match'. Both poem and painting record a moment of innocence (lost innocence, of course, in the case of, 'Going to the Match') in the relationship between a town and its sporting heroes. That the professional era in the rugby world has seen a dramatic decline in Hawick's fortunes, gives to 'An Auld "Dye" ' too, something of a 'Remembrance of Things Past' quality. Neither poem nor painting, however, has lost point or relevance.

'The Vertish' is one of David Hill's best-known poems. Basically light-hearted, it yet bears on the mutability of human affairs, in a way that will resonate strongly with most of its readers. The rueful stanza-ending lines are arrived at after a satisfyingly involved journey through the streets and prospects of the poet's West End.

Ye may ken, I was born and bred i' The Loan
In a yin-end whunstane biggin'
Wi' an oot-look on to the Bleachin' Green
And Back-Brae craws on the riggin';
A guid-gaun lum for a wunter's nicht,
Wi' my feet on the polished fender –
But they cam' and condemned it, and garred mei flit –
Mei! A born Wast-ender!

The 'Dutch interior' touches in this opening stanza, remind us that in 'Ripeness is All' (included in this volume) the poet pays an elegant tribute to the art of Rembrandt.

From the more specifically 'Hawick' poems we return briefly to the general body of Scots work. 'Scab' illustrates David Hill's very sure instinct for the word which is, in the context of the poem, both surprisingly, and incontrovertibly right.

Up the Manse glebe
Where the brae bends sweet,
Was sic a fraith o' scab
As ca'd a halt to my feet.

Fient anither floo'er there
Naething mair, nor less,
Than the swing o' the road
Throwe the lang swayin' gress.

"Sweet", and "swing", make of the road an almost living presence amongst the quietly, but intensely visualized wild parsley, the 'Scab' of the title.

In the English poems we find the same observant eye, and distinctively individual voice we have come across in the vernacular poetry. 'East Anglia - 1940-41' takes us back to that odd, suspenseful time, when against the background of the tremendous, inescapable, presence of the War, life went on in a way both real and unreal. It exemplifies again the poet's rare ability to let us in on that conversation going on below the conversation, of which Neil M. Gunn has written, and which derives so much of its potency from being heard at one remove. We could read 'East Anglia' straightforwardly as a nature poem, but we do not.

> In this ripe and stagey season
> Melancholy is born on every wind.
> . . . A treacherous time
> When from the inside of the window shows
> An innocent snail-gallop of scalloped clouds
> Strung across the sky as in summer days.
> But going out-doors the air is edged, and the wind
> An importunate demon.

'East Anglia' is war poetry of the first order; the stage-set that was Southern England in those fateful years can rarely have been better evoked. In that very striking image, "An innocent snail-gallop of scalloped clouds", the first words have the ominous undertone proper to "A treacherous time."

'In November' is another memorable dispatch from one of history's pivotal turning-points. The harvest has come and gone

> And over stubbled acres
> Moves an uneasy air,
> A wind from outer dark, swinging pair by pair
> The gape-mouth bells in the flinty tower
> That tongue no more for God.

That "uneasy", echoes in a strange and powerful way, a passage in Rudyard Kipling's Romney Marsh poem, 'The Dykes'.

> So we come down, uneasy, to look;
>   uneasily pacing the beach.
> These are the dykes our fathers made:
>   we have never known a breach.

Against this background the poet on 'Leave in March' sees with a lucid intensity the unchanging miracles of nature, and the beauty of the suddenly so precarious common day. In the garden are

Crocuses, bright as blown flame . . .
Lupin leaves like tiny green hands . . .
A worm jewelled with sunlight, butting and retracting
after being turned up by the spade.

David Hill's fluent and idiomatic prose style, always at ease with the subject and itself, is seen to much advantage in the prose items included in this volume. 'A Matter of Time', and 'Too Hot for Candles', both fifteen minute pieces broadcast by the B.B.C., are very ingeniously constructed murder mystery stories. The consummately professional handling of dialogue can keep two persons graphically there on the page with a mere "What's that?" "Wad ye like to hear it? What's that? Och no . . . I'm in nae hurry sir" ('A Matter of Time'). The percipient dictum that less is more, is finely illustrated by the easy assurance of the opening sentence of "Too Hot for Candles' - "Of course there was never any real need for me to work at all." No tedious setting of the scene here; as with masters like Chandler (though naturally, David Hill's 'entertainment' only very briefly invites such a heavyweight comparison) we plunge straight into the story, marching stride by stride, so to say, with the narrator as he gathers and develops his thoughts.

'Centenary' is the third fifteen minute B.B.C. piece reproduced here. It has the confident narrative marshalling of its sister stories, and it has an additional interest in that it appears to feature the author as literary critic and social commentator. The poet, a sort of not quite mute inglorious Milton, whose 1896 book of verses, 'Starcleuch Edge', prompts our narrator to an idiosyncratic act of commemoration, is differentiated sharply from the omnipresent "bardies . . . and their sonsy, flat-footed muse". Unlike them, John Caverton is "un-pawky". 'Starcleuch Edge' is not disfigured by a "belly-crawling dedication to some laird who had promised to take a dozen copies." It is a pleasure to meet Mr William Sudden of the 'Border Sentinel'. His affable but resolute refusal to find room in his columns for a few commemorative comments on the rather tragic poet, is very deftly conveyed.

'Thirty-Six Hours' is a fine study of a man at the end of his tether, first emotionally, and then both emotionally and physically, as he waits for the news which will put to rest his deep anxieties about his wife and unborn, but imminently expected child. Fraught as much of the story is, it has, certainly not uncharacteristically, the odd highly amusing moment.

As a Castilian hidalgo of ninety-five quarterings,
I regret that I am unable to pay my state visit on
a horse . . . something . . . something . . . an unusually
wet season . . . equestrian exercise is impracticable.

Look out for the repetition of that last half-sentence several pages on, when the physical crisis resultant on his nightmarish bout of cramp in a fuselage space "fourteen inches by twelve", has just past, and the emotional crisis moves towards its resolution.

David Hill is a 'new contributor' to 'The Penguin New Writing No. 19 October – December 1944'. Among the 'old hands' who feature alongside him in the issue are Louis MacNeice, and W.H. Auden.

'Chucks-Mei!', carries the sub-title, 'A Choice of Pleasures, People and Places'. First published in the Transactions of the Hawick Archaeological Society for 1957, it is an extended ramble through matters linguistic, literary, social and historical. It includes poems by the author and friends, a very judicious and balanced consideration of the career of Thomas Boston, the Calvinist minister of Ettrick, and a very well told account of the first African voyage of Mungo Park.

A number of poems, Scots and English, document David Hill's responses to painting and music. In 'Renoir's "La Loge" ', characteristically displaying that command of metre and rhyme, subversive of conventional expectations, he contemplates roses. In the painting they

> Drop, drifflin, frail doon
> To their mortal lair.
> But Renoir's roses.
> And lovely frail Mimi,
> Hersel a rose, though langsyne dust,
> Will aye be there.

If he hoped for his own art – as 'Withy-Basket' seems to suggest he did – a modest immortality, he surely did not do so in vain.

> All I have ever done is to make withy-baskets
> of words . . .
> in the hope that somewhere
> there was somebody who would say
> "I am glad, I am sure, because I remember it was so."

The present volume would not have come into being had Mrs Ina Scott Hill, the poet's wife, not preserved with every care and attention, the original texts, against the day to which she so much looked forward, when her husband's work could be published in due and fitting form. Very sincere thanks are owed to Mrs Frances Paxton for her most exact and painstaking work in preparing fresh and exemplary copies for the printers.

The comprehensive glossary of the Scots words featured in the poems, provided at the end of the volume, reflects the very considerable expertise of Mr Norman Turnbull in this area. The fine 1934 'Caricature Portrait' is by the late Mr Malcolm Nicholson, a family friend. Very warm congratulations are due to Mr David Andrew Hill, the poet's son, and to Hawick Callants' Club, for the initiative which has now made readily accessible, between these covers, a notably distinguished contribution to modern Scottish literature.

Hugh K. Mackay.

"AIN GATE"

HAWICK & BORDERS

THE VERTISH

Ye may ken, I was born and bred i' the Loan,
In a yin-end whunstane biggin',
Wi' an ootlook on to the Bleachin' Green
And Back-Brae craws on the riggin';
A guid-gaun lum for a wunter's nicht,
Wi' my feet on the polished fender –
But they cam' and condemned it, and garred mei flit –
Mei! A born Wast-ender!

I work away i' the spinnin'-mill
Up to the cuits in ooder.
But I'm fain for a sicht o' the Vertish Hill
Wi' his plaid flung owre his shooder.
His waistcoat and breeks o' comely green,
The wud hei weers like a croon.
And I mind o' the days that yince hae been
And my hert's sair cuissen-doon.

For now o' The Loan that I used to ken
There's hardly a stannin' stane;
Even my douce auld neebor The Moat
Looks muckle to mean and lane –
But **hei** has the Vertish to bield his back,
And keep things a' in order . . .
There's higher hills? Aye! But where'll ye sei
A bonnier view o' the Border?

Man . . . Ocht worth tippence gaun on i' the toon
Aye comes there, sune or later –
Cornets and Callants and mairchin' bairns –
It's a local law o' Natur' !
Golfers and sledgers and dydie-eggs,
Or auld folk seekin' a sate
O' a simmer's nicht, the Hill's aye there
And his welcome never blate.

So . . . juist dinna let-on if ye sei mei nod
Guid-nicht, to my freend owre thonder
As dowie I gang for the Burnfit bus
For mony's the time I ponder
How is't that yon humphie-backit hicht
Can steer up thochts sae tender?
For there's never a hill like the Vertish Hill
To a guitter-bluid Wast-ender!

AT EASTER

I was ta'en, I mind, as a laddie
Wha neither kent nor cared,
To see auld Dauvit's heidstane
In a lirk o' St. Mary's Yaird.

Lang and mony a day syne...
And little it meant to me,
A bairn wha thocht on a twalmonth
As near an eternity.

But yin blythe Easter morning
I bo'ed to see his stane
Yince mair, and took my callant,
Hauf-sweir, to ken his ain.

Owre sune for Sunday papers,
Bye wundas blank and still,
We hand in hand thegither
Clam' up the green kirk-hill.

Auld names, lost days forgotten,
Peered oot frae raw by raw,
Flakin' or bleared wi lichen,
Weariet and fain to fa'.

Past Sprot, we gaed, and Nixon,
Stitt, Lockup, Summers, Swan,
Whale, Mars, Domone, and Moscrip,
Hislop and Harraman,

Past spinster, spouse, and relict,
Past flesher, wabster, hind,
And the nameless host o' infancy
Nane but mithers wad mind,

Until we cam' to Dauvit,
And I helped the bairn to spell
The deep-cut lettering that showed
The same name as himsel'.

Stravaigin' thochts beset me:
How forty 'eer had passed
Yet strengthening ties o' kinship
Had brocht me back at last.

Dauvit had dwalt i' the Mid Raw
And plied wi' his cairrier cairt
Jinglin' raig'lar ilk a week
Owre-bye the Copshaw airt.

Ca'in his pownies throwe fair and foul
By the clints o' Robert's Linn,
He throve frae seeventeen-fifty-five
And leeved to be echty-yin.

Weel he wad ken Wull Gotterson
Wi' his strampin' ootsteek shoon,
And heard the ridin' ballads
'Or Scott ere wrote them doon.

Trocked, whiles, wi' smuggled brandy –
Unless I dae him wrang –
Whiles drank a stowp wi' Dandie,
And saw the yeomen thrang

To quell the Frainch invasion
When the false beacons glared....
Then I mindit, sudden, o' the bairn,
And wondered how he fared.

But he sat close ahint me,
His bricht een dancin' gleg,
Crying' "Shairly it must be time, now,
To trinnle my dydie egg!"

And so, abune auld Dauvit,
We played an aulder game,
There in the airly stillness,
Till it was time for hame.

Past Sprot, we gaed, and Nixon,
Stitt, Lockup, Summers, Swan,
Whale, Mars, Domone, and Moscrip,
Hislop and Harraman.

And saw the sun o' Easter
Heeze up and lowe until
It kinnled till a burnin' buss
The thorns on Hardie's Hill.

GABLE-END

I watched the deliberate
Last Destruction o Wulton
Yin simmer Setterday afternune.
Wulton was biggit in comely stane
Quarried frae native hills –
Frei-stane and whun…

And I saw a bull-dozer
Bashin at a fower –fit gable
O' whun. Bashin. And gaun back.
And bashin. And aye the whun,
Wi mortar mixed wi Tei'ot grevel –
Sma, sma stanes; a study their-sel –
Aye the whun stude: dour shoodert,
Waitin for the next daud…..

And there cam to my mind,
Watchin this odds on duel
Wi a machine that was bund
To wun i' the end, the thocht
O' auld mason-tredsmen
Lang-syne deid, that built,
And built weel wi this thrawn stane
Sae like their-sels –mebbe watchin,
And allowin' this fecht
Atween their creative hand-work
And a destructive stinkin deevil,
And cheerin' on that auld gable-end –
The Last Wulton Resistance –
Cheerin' like hell! But kenning.

Aa went away, wae,
For auld crafts and lost skills
Afore it cam daudin' doon.

STOCKING MAKERS

The guid auld days: The twalmonth

Chapped in twae
Atween the Common Riding
And the New 'Eer –
Twae six month stints o cuddy-work
Slockened wi drams and yill.

Yet their mirry memorials
Where they stand their state
Arena in modest stones
In Wulton and Walligate –
But mansions stan split
 doon the middle, now –
On Sunnyhill.

“ROBBIE DYE”

A Bothy Ballad.
For the information of a visitor who heard the Hawick supporters shouting, and said “Whae was Robbie Dye?” And dedicated, with the greatest respect, to the memory of the real owner of the nickname, whose only resemblance to the character described below lay in his devotion to the game of (Hawick) Rugby Football.

Come a’ you lads o’ the Borderland
That follow the Rugby game,
And I’ll tell ye o’ a Hawick man
Weel kent to local fame;
He wasna born like yow or mei,
And I’ll tell ye the reason why:
He juist poppit oot a duffle-bag
So they ca’d him Robbie dye.

His faither workit at the mill
Like mony a decent chap,
And he brocht hame some jerseys
The bairnie for to hap;
It girned at the red, and grat at the blue –
But it gied a joyfu’ cry,
And grup ahaud o’ the green yin,
So they christened him Robbie Dye.

When Robbie first went to the schule
At sums he was richt dour,
And the teacher said, “If ye canna coont,
Ye’ll never can tell the score:
Now if Gala had threi penalty goals,
And Hawick but a single try,
Whae wad ye say had won, my lad?”
- “The referee,” says Dye.

Then he fell frae grace at the Sunday Schule
For tellin them Noah’s Ark
Was muckle aboot the same for size
As the stand at Mansfield Park.
“And where,” they speired, “is the Promised Land?”
He answered-up, richt spry,
“Juist haud strecht doon bye the Gas Works,
And ye’re there,” says Robbie Dye.

Rob aye played scrum-half as a boy,
Wi’ a service fast and shair,
But never grew bigger than fower-fit-ten

And the loss to the game was sair!
He'd a bonny cut-throwe on Mansfield Brig,
And away, like a blue-tailed fly
Past the Sew'rage gate, if he thocht he was late
Went supersonic Dye!
Week oot, week in, Rob followed the team
Wherever they chanced to play;
His wunter began efter Langholm Sports
And his simmer on New 'Eer's Day.
A' the rest was a waste o' time
Till the back-end o' July,
When he saw it was suner derk at nicht;
- "Oo're gettn't in!" says Dye.

Now Rob hed but yin ambition in life –
It wasna like askin' much –
Owr' sma' to play or to referee:
Juist yince to rin the touch.
"If only I could, juist yince," he pled
Wi every "heid-yin" nigh,
Till, at last, in a game o' the Border League,
They handit the flag to Dye!

O, never a Cornet as prood as Rob
Ever breistit the Nipknowes Brae,
As he trottit aboot on his short bit legs,
Watchin' the rin o' play!
But – he tripped on the straw as a wheelin' maul
Swung roond like a herd o' kye,
And sixteen forrits o' thirteen stane
Cam' doon on the top o' Dye!

When they sortit the muddle oot at last,
The lassies grat and roared,
For there lay Dye – still haudin' his flag –
But as flat as a hosiery-board!
The doctor that cam' to gie him aid
Juist shook his heid wi' a sigh,
And then, i' the hush as they cairriet him off,
A whisper cam' frae Dye:

"I dinnae want buriet in Wulton, boys,
For although it's faisable near,
I'd never ken o' a meenit's peace
When I heard them roar and cheer.
And I couldna fancy the Walligate:
It's fer owre fer ootbye . . . .
So ye'd mebbe be better to cremate
The remains o' puir Robbie Dye."

"And scatter my ashes yonder, boys,
Where they'll get weel daudit-in,
On the shundered bank where the Robbies stand
And chaff, and champ their shuin;
And though players come and players go,
Wi my last braith I'll prophesy –
They may fade away, when they've had their day,
But there'll aye be a Robbie Dye!"

So if, at the Sports, ye've said "A' that I care
Is to see the best seeven wun."
- Then offered your specs to the referee
- Or the first tie was weel begun;
- Then argyed "off-side" wi a Gala man
Till he tellt ye to gang Doon-bye-
But lookit sae vexed when his team got bate
That ye gied him half your pie . . . .

If you couldna swally the tother half,
Though ye'd hed the denner at yin,
And chowed your programme to bits insteed,
Till the Final was a' but dune . . . .
Lost your bonnet, and a' that was left o' your voice,
As the Greens got the wunnin' try . . . .
Then, take my word, ye're "gey-hard-up,"
For the symptons never lie:
He's hed ye! Ye're hit! Ye've gotten the smit! Ye're <u>another</u> Robbie Dye.

SANDSTANE SODGER

(The South African War Memorial statue; smashed by a gale on 12th January, 1974.)

Yon sandstane sodger was unveiled
By Lord Roberts, seeventy eer syne.
They a' strutted aboot like cockerels,
In gold braid, scarlet, and feathery hats.
And when proper respect had been paid,
And a' the patriotic oratory dune,
They went away – nae doot to wine and dine –
And left him to guaird the names.

Twa-threi gentry, and a wheen callants
Are commemorated there – deid o dysantry,
Mauser bullets, or gangrene,
In a sordid little war ….
And I've aye had a feeling that yon sodger
Was wonderin what it had a' been aboot,
But naebody'd made him as wice.

Seeventy eer's a lang time to stand guard,
Wonderin what it was for…
And only the pipes can say, in lament,
How it's aye the young lost deid we honour:
Never a war.

BIRTH-PLACE

"Here 'Old Mortality' was born"
Says the lettered stane bune the sma
Conventicle o' hens that bide,
This nicht o' Februar thaw,
Hoose-room at Haggis-ha.

The covened airs o' derkenin steer
Aboot the steedin, pad and paw;
Murnin in tongues man kent afore
His first word was let-fa,
They keen and souch and blaw,

Dirlin daized casements, still, wi the roll
O' Dunnottar's hirdit deid, and a'
The hodden names on stanes that tilt
Forfochen on muir and law,
But he's lang beyond their ca,

Nor comes in a lantern-haar o' braith
Cryin "Haud!" to the reckonin they draw:
Siccar the slow, slow fingers rub,
Straikin withoot staw,
Smoorin his name on the wa.

FISH RINNIN

It's nocht like what it used to be
I doot I'm getting auld,
There's no' a sowl to be seen now
Doon at the cauld.
The wund and the rain's been roarin'
Thir twae nichts and mair,
The water's lippin, bank and brae,
But naebody's there –
Fish rinnin, fishin rinnin,
And naebody there!

Mebbe the bailies hae gotten owre fly;
Mebbe a dram's owre dear,
And the price at mony a douce back-door
Buy's only beer.
And what guid's that for shorkin feet?
Blashy stuff, I'm shair,
For its chitterin work wi cleek and stick,
But naebody's there.
Fish rinnin, fish rinnin,
And naebody there!

Mebbe they've a' gien up at last
And taen to catchin troots,
Mebbe they're even workin –
But I hae my doots!
What wad they dae workin,
Wi the sough o the flude i the air,
Derk fins slittin the slide o the cauld,
Yet naebody's there.
Fishin rinnin, fish rinnin,
And naebody there!

Mebbe … mebbe they're a' deid;
I'm nane owre gleg mysel.
Whiles they wad look gey shilpit
When the wund was snell.
Aye … But what's yon – Jock! – Tam!
Andra! - twae-three mair.
Look … Owre yonder. D'ye see him?
Ten, toonty pund, I'm shair.
Fish rinnin, fish rinnin
Enough and to spare!

Weekly Scotsman Nov 6, 1952

“IN – COMERS!”

(For J.E.)

The roads atween Hawick
And Langholm
Are the roads atween
Heaven and hell,

Wi’ The ‘Paul as a bieldy
Limbo
Where the lost drooths
Dwell,

But whutch road-en’s
Whutch, or the tother,
Only the tribes
Can tell.

R.K.D.

(For Robert Domingo)

Och, Robert, lad…juist days syne I was gi'en
A pickle Smith's fifteen-eer Glenlivet
For my birthday. And I meant to share wi ye
It's peat-reeky, granite-water swirlin
O' delectable speerit; it's illumination
O' the droll frailties o the human race –
'Livened wi weel-exampled ribaldry! –
But now ye're gane.
 And your epic
O' auld Henry and his lost battle
Atween the medicine and Barclay's yill
Gan a' unrecorded but in bruckle memory.

Wild-flo'oers, blood-stock, Border lore, bird-sang,
Rough logic, prejudices, courtesy –
Your foibles were a' your ain.
Stoic at the end, tholin' your paiks;
My hert's a hivvy stane,
Drinkin' this dram, alane.

BORDER TERRIERS 1
(both for Roy Thomson)

Gin I'd a bit mair
O' worldly riches,
And needna work a' day,
I think I wad keep
Threi Border bitches
To haud auld Time at Bay.

And they wad hev hides
Like benty gress;
Yin blue, mebbe twae reid grizzle,
Wi' the blunt otter heid,
And abune ocht else,
The black and blaggarty muzzle.

And they wad worry
Imaigined rats, sweirin
Oaths I daurna name,
Yet lick my luif
Richt tenderly
When I cam weariet hame.

BORDER TERRIERS 2

This young yin's kind
Like a' her kind:
Comes waggin, mad,
And lickin, warm,
Like ony whalp I've ever kent –
And that's owre mony.

Puir beast, she's workin hard
At succession. But the auld yin
We hed to pit doon…
In her latter days hed nae need
To lick or wag. Everything
Was in her fond filmed een
And we baith kent
Time was rinnin oot…..

This whalp, weel
She's weel enough, nae doot,
But it's the callant
She heels aboot…

Why should yin's life
Be measured, name on name,
By a tale of terriers.

THE BLEACH

(In Memoriam)

The "Bleach" was the communal bleaching or drying green situated between the Moat Park and Drumlanrig School, part of which has now been used for the school buildings.

Weel, can I mind o' The Bleach and the wild
Ballet o' weshins on blawy Spring Mondays;
The gibbous balloonin goonies o' grannies,
The daft cavortin o' combinations, the sprig jig
O' bairns, sma-claes, snawy streets o' sheets
And boulevards o' blankets ruggin an rivin'
At the grey, grainin ranks o' poles that leaned
Hauf-dazed, like deef auld men, listenin.

Listenin wi' battered lugs to births an' daiths
And lang, decades o' forgotten scandals
Mummled throwe moothfu's o' claes-pins
By guid-wives, crouse wi' saip's salvation
Twae Sunday sermons ahint them and the deevil dirt
Sent roarin yince again in a smother o' graith
Doon the cundies o' The Loan.

An' weel I can mind o' toddlin' to The Bleach
Yin distant simmer's day, wi' a biscuit in my hand,
Fresh frae the lang mysterious spicy drawer
O' the Store Van – waled, efter an agony's choice
While the muckle horse snorted, clattin the causays
And the slow steam o' new-bakit breid
Oozed throwe the slats, and the van-man hotched
And hotched at his leather pooch, waitin' to change my penny.

The gress grew lang and leish ahint the schule,
Lang gress wi' feathery tops that tickled my chin
As I waded deep there that simmer efternune.
There were butterflies to chase, gresshoppers chirred,
An' buirdly bummies pub-crawled in the clover.
A thoosand butter-cups waited to confirm
Yin's likin for butter, and the insect world
Hummed wi' a busyness that became a creddle-song
And I sat-doon at last wi' daisies in my lap.

"Two ones are two. Two twos are four –"
The drowsy plain-chant cam yawnin' throwe
The open wundaes o' the Schule. Heavy wi' denners
And heat, the scholars dreamed o' The Dunk
And Coble – "Two twos are four" they droned.

I fummled wi the bricht daisies splittin'
Their sappy stems, clumsily stringin' twae, threi
Or fower - "Two twos are four" confirmed the class
Singin' me nearer and nearer to sleep –

Why should yin bother at this time o' day
To write o' a bairn hover-doverin' in The Bleach?
I set it doon for mindin' to ony bairn that took
His steps, yince, to yon green and quiet place –
Or ony plot o' lost peace and innocence;
But mair in maimory o' gentle hands
That wakened me, and a kindliness that knew
The hairst o' deid that simmer on The Somme
An yet had patience to coont ower to me
The daisies on my cheen.

Wars come
A' in their ain wersh time. In my bairn's world
It only felt cooler now. Douce as a curny dumplin'
Sat The Moat. And the scholars had reached
Rare hichts o' multiplyin', and fa'n still at last –
For want o' braith or lear. A train cam clinkin doon,
Snakin' atween the Slitrig hills. And the dark shadows
O' the poles lay felled and lang athort The Bleach,
The green gress o' The Bleach, now gane.

A FISHER'S LULLABY

Aa've putten away the wand
And Aa'm airtin for bed,
Mindin-owre the mony
Guid fishin-days Aa've hed.

Bonnie troots a-plenty
Hae frizzled in my pan:
Some Aa wad keep
And some Aa'd let gaun.

But thaim Aa forget
(Aa'm thinkin, wi a yawn)
Are thaim that Aa ett,
No' thaim Aa let gaun,

And 'tween thaim Aa let gaun,
And the yins that got away,
Lies a lang taingled story
Aa'll tell ee some day.
Aye, …. Some other day ….

GHAISTS

JOCK O THE PAIRK

(Newcastleton station was built on the site of 'Little Jock' Elliot's residence)

Jock's ghost cam yammerin
Yammerin doon
Fu o indignation
For on the site o his strang to'er
They built a railway station ......

Trains uffed and puffed
For mony an 'eer
But, i' the end, the nation
Decided (per yon Richard Marsh)
Rail had nae destination:
And now, auld Jock and
Auld ghost trains
Share spectral assignation, -
At Copshaw station!

Note:
There is a strong rumour that when the railway re-opens, the first train north from Carlisle has been chartered by Armstrongs International in conjunction with Elliots Incorporated, and the first yin oot at Copshaw Station that can prove hei didna steal his ticket, dog, bacca-pooch or his neebor's serk, gets the freedom of Liddesdale.

TIMING

Sae, naething laith
hei drank it slowly doon-
His last drop o' maut licker-
But gin hei'd hained
The odd hauf-croon
Hei wad hae druckent quicker!

GREAT UNCLE WULL

The bare banes o' this tale cam' frae
a Cannobie wumman in Australia, mindin' o' auld times

Great-uncle Wull at Copshaw Holm,
Wha dealt in swine and kye,
Relished 'bune ony butcher-meat,
A denner o' craw-pie.

And to this end, his ancient gun,
A' spring-time without fail,
Roared murder throwe ilk merdit wud
The length o' Liddesdale,

Spreidin' aboot the primrose shaws
Daith, hurt, and raucous fear,
The auld to rot, the young for the pot,
Till gaun on his nintieth eer –

When yin day, guzzlin' at a pie,
The fand him, a' his lane,
Black i' the face as a damson ploom
And chowkit on a bane.

They buried Wull at Ettleton
Where a' his kindred lay,
But few there were to follow him
For he'd lang oot'-leeved his day,

His neffa Rob, and twae-threi hirds,
A drover frae Langtoon,
Syne greetin' sair, and on the stot,
Puir drucken Airchie Broon.

But or they'd weel won-throwe the yett,
A ferlie they did see –
Naething but scoores and scoores o' craws
On every kirkyaird trei;

Hiddlin' close, wi' never a soond,
Watchin' wi' bead-bricht een,
Till the prayers were said, and Wull was laid
Aneth the sod sae green.

Then, at the benediction's end,
As he turned to pit on his tile,
Even the minister had to cough
To cover owre a smile;

For a' the craws rase up at yince
In a cawin' cloud o' joy,
And off to their native wuds to tell
The end o' a life-lang ploy,

That auld Wull's bleezin blunderbuss
Was silent now, at last,
And craws, frae Steele to Liddlebank,
Micht ken their skaith was past;

To Sorbietrees and Larriston,
Wi' news that Wull was deid,
And craws micht leave in peace at last
Frae Flatt to Tweeden-heid . . .

But Wull's departure brocht, alas!
Nae glad millennium,
For Copshaw craws still take the same
Auld road to kingdom-come,

Gleanin' what little comfort's gaun
Frae the cauldrife compromise
That though as mony as ever get shot,
There's fewer get baked in pies.

And drucken Airchie swore, life-lang,
Wull's funeral was the best
Attendit that he'd ever seen -
And the maist faisable dresst.

1/11/1961

<u>THREI HAWICK SONNETS</u>

by DAVID HILL

**Dedicat til a man (syne deid) wha speired:
"Hev ee been writin ony hairy poetry, lately?"**

Mertinmas. 1969.

<u>POACHERS</u>

Where's a' the poachers gane? Yince, yin could tell
At sicht, thon thrissles i the douce kailyaird
We ca society. They never cared
A resh for bailies, polis, or kirk-bell;

Scannin the sleek-back't Cauld; dichtin a mell;
Sookin a fag-end throwe a threi-days' baird;
Daurin the whummlin flude withoot regaird
For ocht, bar rinnin fish, this side o Hell: -

Dae'n time at firesides now; mindin, nae doot,
Auld days, illegal baits, unlawfu gear;

The feel o mushrooms; broilin a gumpit troot;
Pheesant-ploys in black wuds, wi gameys near;

Spring waitter-gates, wi primroses aboot;
Six-month, bleezin, simmers; six-penny beer.

DEGENERAT BREID

Wae-worth yon Plastic Breid that's sellt the-day,
In sliddery greaseproof, wi a fancy name;
Ilk sei-throwe, clatchy, slice the hairs-breedth same.
Nae crusty "door-step" now, and oot to play

Wi try-cle on eer chowks. Better, daur-say,
Brocht factory-fresh (sei telly) til eer hame,
Twae hunder miles, than frae some mercat-krame
Or horse-van, unhygienic as a kay!

Where are yon rowes that garred the hert rejoice?
What wairpit Breid Board said they had to go?

"Skinny" or "grey" – ee even got a choice:
Succulent dauds o lestic-sided dough

That wrocht the jaw-banes, stilled the hungert voice,
And swalled to girdit bliss the void below!

AN AULD "DYE"

Lang-syne, Aa walkit up the waitterside
And owre the Station Brig, efter a game;
But, tell the truith, the legs irna the same
Nowadays. Weel, sin' auld-age wunna hide,

Aa get the bus. Aa fair enjoy thon ride:
Roarin up throwe the Mansfield mirk, for hame;
Chaffin and argyin; clashin oot praise and blame;
Ca-in the ref., and goal-kicks that gaed gleyed!

But sune – owre sune – we're on the bleezin Street.
We stop and stert. The cronies drift awa;

The crack gauns deid. The hindmaist, weariet, feet
Are mine. Yin mair, yin less: that's mortal law;

But won or lost; sunshine or blatterin weet;
How guid it's been, man, seiin them rin the ba!

AUGUST HOLIDAYS

Aa wad say –
Come an oo'll gaun somewhere
The morn. He'd say aye.
Then wadna budge
Frae a walk up the Ludge.

Aa wad say
Is't the money ee grudge?
Hei'd say no.
But hei wadna budge
Frae his walk up the Ludge.

But aa kept on at um
And at last hei grei'd
Wi' a smudge
On a trip to sei the Forth Brig.

But oo slep' in and now
Hei's chowkin' wi' lauchin'
Oor sandwiches an a made ready
For mair
Than a sate up the Ludge.

1973.

SHUNDERT

(Til an Auld Freend, for G.A.)

We've wandert mony a mile
And fer oor peths hae sundert,
But aa mind a day, lang-syne,
Aa met ee at the Vertish edge
Trailin' eer sledge,
And said: "What is't like,
The Nippers? Solid?
"No", ee said,
"Shundert."

But still, up thon weary brae
Onward aa blundert…
Is there a moral to be pykit here?
Aa've whiles wondert.
Aa hed to sei for mysel'
And it was
Shundert…
Mind… Aa wadna dae'd nowadays.
Lod-sakes-mei, no.
Everything's shundert!

PUIR MAGGIE BROON

(A Cautionary Tale)

Ah, puir deludit
Maggie Broon!
She thocht the High Street
Belanged the Toon;

She scrimps gey sair
Her rates to meet,
And so, has a richt
To wun-owre the Street.

In aulder times,
When she was young,
A' she need jouk
War' hotts o dung,

And ca'd them for
A dirty clairt
Frae Mutter Howey's
Horse and cairt....

Sic days are gane,
Alas, lang since –
We dice wi daith
For a pund o mince...

So, Maggie peers
Throwe diesel fumes,
For room to cross
And buy some plooms,

And – she's juist mindit –
Wants, forbye,
To get the auld man's
Denner pie.

But dunneran tyres
And poisoned reek
Chowk her till she
Can hardly speak,

While beer, and breid,
Cats-meat, scrap-caurs,
Pink plastic potties,
Dutch ceegars,

And muckle trucks
O' frozen lamb
Belt off to France
Or Amsterdam.

Malt, saip, and soda,
Sheep and kye,
And bedroom-suites,
Gang birlin bye,

Wi sma regaird
For Hawick toon,
And even less
For Maggie Broon …

Weariet, at last,
O' sic-like scenes,
She risks a'
For a tin o beans -

Riska a', wae's mei!
For beans on toast;
Aa've seen waur
I' "The Sunday Post!"…

Maggie's now up
The Walligate,
(Pairt paid-for
By The Welfare State.)

Neebors: be wairned! –
If ye'd bide leevin –
Let's have Hawick High Street,
No' A.7.

We've yin last chance
To stop this 'gig' …
Sellt doon the river
Owre a brig!

OWRE WHITA

Lang-syne it was,
Thon souchin simmer's day,
Wi' cloods that sailed
Loutin to their shaddas
Like swans briestin the surges
O' breckan. And heather-cowes,
Buddit for besoms, breenged wild
At the back o' the hill.

But aye and anon i' the howes
It was suddenly wundless: stane
Unco stane-still. Wi' a bummie
Ryin fisherman's-basket
Under the hauf-blin stare
O' blaeberries; the universe
Starred wi' un-numbered galaxies
O' tormentil.

Mebbe yon was
A dryer 'eer. For I mind nocht
O' this black ineluctable peat
That drags now at my feet.

(For Ina and Langholm 5/8/1932 con amore 9/12/1975)

ENCOUNTER

I met a man ootbye the muir;
He watcht a rabbit in a snare.

As roon it ran wi stertan een,
A waesome squeal the craiter gien.

To kill or free I forrit ran –
Whan on my shooder was his han'.

"lat be, my lad, e'en lat it be;
For sae rins a' humanity,

"And what's a rabbit's chowkan dance
Compare't wi snares o circumstance,"

Confoondit by philosophy,
I gove't at him, he glowert at me,
And, Ah, he had an eller ee!

1937.

SERKS

Sic orra serks folk wear
Nowadays: pink and blue
Like flashes o electricity!

I can mind when tredsman wore
Flannen serks wi a navy blue stripe.
They were weel-possed wi
Carbolic saip, and weel syndit
And hung-oot for a caller blaw,
Then ernt and weel aired
Afore a roarin' fire o coals,
And putten-on, and tucked-in,
And the sleeves rowed-up,
And the haill ootfit ready,
Complete, comfortable, for a week's work:
Sealed, ye micht say,
Wi' a brass stud, forbye:
And thank God, nae chowkin'
Sunday collar and tie.

<u>'STRANGERS'</u>

Yin Common Ridin mornin
Ma mother says ti mei
"Ee'd better watch eer-sel, lass,
"Here's a 'stranger' in eer tei."

Weel, aa met a lorry-driver,
As smert as ee could sei;
Mebbe hei'd hed a pint or twae
Or even twae or threi;

But hei took iz roond the Haugh –
Oh, how the time did flei!
Then up the Spetch and hed a sate
Ablow thon hawthorn trei.

Hei said they ca'd um Chairlie Broon –
Mind, it could hev been a lei .....
But aa've a little laddie now,
As like um as a pei!

Ma mother was gey roosed –
Till the bairn was on her knei,
"Mam – whae was ma faither?"
"Wheesht, lass…(ee'll hev um wakent)….
Howts - juist a 'stranger' in ma tei."

CURRENCY

Aa want naething else adae
Wi money
Except to sit at the Dunk
And watch the auld currency
Floatin' bye.
Thrippences, tanners, bobs, florins,
The odd halfcroon
Come floatin' doon.
But then we were gien
 in decimal? –
Nae doot but yon
Was aye handy
To a guid risin troot.

END OF AN AULD SANG

(W. & J. Kennedy, Booksellers 1829-1971)

Maybe it is for every generation to feel
The sma tragedy: to have oot-leeved
What it had aye kenned,
And likit weel –

But Maisters Walter and John Kennedy
Have murdered been, by crass
Authority,
For sake o engine-stink
And whudderan wheel

Hawick men yince mairched to Jeddart,
Ettlin to be free:
They wad hae roared to the riggin-heids:
"Iniquity!" . . . .

"So what?" we shrug, and turn the telly on;
Conned and content to let things be;
And The Plans creep, slidderan,
whiter than white,
Frae the brain-washing machine
o Bureaucracy.

31/12/1971

THE SPETCHMAN

(A Spring for the Pipes)

Sae blithe and clear the Spetchman sang,
As bye his haugh the Tei'ot rummle't;
"O! Mony's the mirry mile I've raiked,
And mony a wainch in hey tummle't;
I may be auld, I may be puir,
Nor ever left guid yill untasted,
But this I ken for certain shair –
A day frae Hawick's a day wasted!"

"The shilfies frae the buskit thorn
Sing salutation to the simmer;
I join their praise by Tei'ot's stream –
What maitter gin' my tune be timmer.
Guid fortune never cam' my airt.
But, faith, I neither socht nor chased it
Throwe drumly foreign dub and clairt-
A day frae Hawick's a day wasted!"

"My fishin-wand, is strang and leish
And troots that i' the Tei'ot tipple,
Like siller muntybanks they spring
When'er I cast oot owre the ripple.
I'll hae them fried in guid yit-meal,
I'll heck them brandered, broiled, or basted,
For here's a truith to shame the deil –
A day frae Hawick's a day wasted!"

"Yon kitchen-lass at Wulton Ludge
Lilts bonny in her harden daidle;
The lad that howes the Lum-Back neeps,
Richt cheerily he plies the paidle;
And caller-clear rins Tei'ot, where
Kind Providence sae wicely placed it;
I'll bide content and canty there –
A day frae Hawick's a day wasted!"

ENVIRONMENT IN OCTOBER

Crisp on auld crisp-bags, slow leaves fa',
The year's golden wonder, happin' them a':
Ham, Cheese'n'onion, vinegar flavour,
Wi' built-in saut that's spent its savour.

'Kung-fuey,' 'Whatsits,' 'Rock'n'Roll,
A buckled beer-can cryin' 'Skol!'
Yin champagne-cork, left for the lawin',
By a Pipe Band efter yon drummin' and blawin'.

A gurly wund beginnin' its capers
Wi' lolly-sticks, beech-nuts, caramel-wrappers,
A Bitter Lemon sighs 'No Return'
To plastic beakers, hauf-fow i' the burn.

Leaves and leavin's beddin' doon;
Whumlin' river, Twilit toon.
'News o' the World' in an empty bin,
And the siller horn o' the Hunter's Mune.

7 /1 /77

POST OFFICE KNOWE

Whae named yon hill-top 'Post Office Knowe',
Fer frae the haunts o' men,
Oot-bye Craik Cross, abune Borthwick-heid?
- I'd fairly like to ken.

And whae brings the letters to Post Office Knowe,
Sae fer frae the haunts o' men?
A whaup wheels roond the pillar-box cairn
Cryin' 'I dinna ken.'

Whae reads a' the cotton-gress postcairds there,
Sae fer frae the haunts o' men?
A black-faced yowe looks up frae her bite
Beh-in' 'I dinna ken.'

They've a tod for telegraph-boy, nae doot,
Sae fer frae the haunts o' men,
And the grey hill-brock draws his pension there,
For ocht I ken.

The telephone linesman's a laverock there,
Fer frae the haunts o' men,
As he spiels up and doon his ledder o' sang,
Blithely, I ken.

But . . . whae's postmaister on Post Office Knowe,
Sae fer frae the haunts o' men?
The wund gangs reeshlin' throwe the bents
Cryin' 'I dinna ken . . . I dinna ken . . .
'Unless it's… Auld Nickie Ben.'

A COUNTRY FIDDLER

Airchie o' the Reuch Sike, ready for the set-tae,
Wi blunt auld fingers calloused frae the howe,
Nid-nid-noddin', and the haill nicht afore him,
A hankie at his chowks and a thick-broon chowe,
Nid-nid-noddin', and the merry fit tappin',
The merry fit tappin', that's quiet, now.

Airchie o' the Reuch Sike, scartin' Drops o' Brandy,
The whaups a' beddit, and ilk lamb and yowe,
Snug aneth the staur-licht, the haill nicht afore him,
A gill inside his serk and a glint on his powe,
Nid-nid-noddin', and the merry fit tappin',
Airchie o' the Reuch Sike, gallus auld Airchie,
The lang nicht afore him, now.

FISHERS? - HECH!

Twas in the month of fair July,
When burns rin sma, and troot are fly
And fishers that wad win a prize
Maun supplicate on bended kneis;
Threi men set forth, withoot a care,
Tae try a cast up Eskdalemuir.
Fishers? – hech!

At Linhope farm – a thousand deils!
A sheep rins in below the wheels.
So richt away, we got aa reckon
A bigger kill than oo's expeckin.
We "laid her doon wi' mickle care,"
And cairrit on tae Eskdalemuir.
Fishers? – hech!

Syne we arrived at Langholm toon
And paid a veesit tae "The Croon"
But, here and now, let it be said,
We didna try their lemonade.
We had ae drink – ae drink – nae mair,
And cairrit on tae Eskdalemuir.
Fishers? – hech!

The road was rough and unco steep,
Enough take make an angel weep.
"Haud on!" says Jock, "it's no' fer now."
The driver only said "Eh whow!"
And then, ten miles thrae onywhere,
We had arrived at Eskdalemuir!
Fishers? – hech!

Cloud shadows chased across each hill,
We thrashed the water wi' a will
The river dimpled ower its stanes,
But we got naething for oor pains.
Thinks I, "The troots maun leeve on air,
That haunt the hags up Eskdalemuir."
Fishers? – hech!

But then oor luck began tae turn
We thocht we'd try yon wee bit burn
And shair enough – w' cry o' wonder –
Oot comes a nice fat quarter-punder!
Which shows yin never should despair,
Even when fishin' up Eskdalemuir.
Fishers? – hech!

At every pule the tale's the same,
And yin mair nice yin tae oor name.
But evening shades were getherin' fast
And aye the next wad be the last.
We fished until oor een grew sair,
(It's derk o' nichts up Eskdalemuir!)
Fishers? – hech!

Then doon the burn we make oor tracks
The baskets bumpin' at oor backs.
The last sheep cryin' thrae the fauld,
The afterglow duist turnin' cauld.
O' ae thing we were certain, shair.
We wad be back at Eskdalemuir!
Fishers? heck!

1932.

THE COMMON GOOD

(to the Anvil Crew Tune)

The Chief Exec. says we should expec'
The rough wi the smooth to share . . . .
O! Hassendean needs a Provost's Cheen
And Jedfit wants Hawick Muir!
For we've had relief frae Lilliesleaf
And subs frae Stobiecote,
So we canna grudge a slice o' the Ludge,
And Minto needs The Moat.

Chorus:
O' The District Lift gauns up and doon,
Oor lum-heids daurna reek,
The cups o tei come roond a' day,
And the scaffies yince a week!

Up at Shankend they're roond the bend
For want o' dacent drains,
There's nae door-knobs inbye for Stobs
And Riccarton needs trains.
At Tei'othead they're sair in need
O' a green where they can putt,
And Mosspaul has nae Public Hall
And so they want The Hut!

Chorus:

So hip-hoorray! Let's gie away
To a that care to come,
An empty mill or the Vertish Hill –
But keep yin fife and drum.
They're scarce o rent for the Provost's Tent
Wi neither a nip nor dram:
Oor Common Good, that Time withstood
It's doon the District Dam!

Chorus:

A HAWICK LADDIE

(from 'Queen o' a' the Border', 1952 BBC Home Service Broadcast from Hawick Town Hall)

Hawick's a grand place to be a laddie in!
Oot on a simmer morning wi the airly sun in eer een,
Wi sparras cheepin gleg on the rones, the cocks crawin,
And the blackies whusslin owre a' the braes and gairdens!

To feel the caller air, and see Cauldcleuch and Skelfhill
Stan'in green and steadfast again' the skyline,
Weel-kenned as the face o' a trusted freend,
Penchrise and Gritmuir, Ruberslaw, dark wi waist-high heather,
And the slant, green, edge o' the Cairter Bar.

Away owre i' the wast, Ettrick Pen, raxin abune his neebors,
And the muckle roond shooders o' the Moffat Hills –
Still, mebbe, wi a glint o late snaw in the deepest cleuchs.

Quiet hills . . . whaup-haunted. . .
        wi burns dernin below deep hags,
Wi cule sphagnum moss to shork atween bare broon taes,
Blaeberries. . and sun and cloud driftin
        and dappling hight and howe.

And aye in the backgrund the music o' rinnin water –
O' Teviot, Slitrig, Borthwick. . . river sangs that bide a lifetime
In a man's lugs, comin back to him in tropical nichts
Under mosquito nets, enticing him throwe the roar o' traffic
In great cities . . . weavin' throwe fitfu'
        dreams in a slit-trench. . .

Drawin' him back. . . .

Hawick's a grand place to be a laddie in!
Wi hill and muir, stream and wud, rain and sun. . .
The exiles weary to come back,
But we who are here, we're exiles tae. . . exiles o' time
If no' o' place. It's a waesome thocht, is't no?
But grand to think back on, juist the same . . .
The Haugh at the Common Riding . . . Hobby-horse days!
Sailin roond in a sea o' bliss wi a coconut in yin hand
And a 'lestic ba' in the tother . . .
        and seeven magic pennies
Still in eer pooch!

GUESS WHAE?

Hei gauns to shoot, up Eskdalemuir,
Was in his time a rugby-player.
Ser' in his scrum throwe foul and fair,
Was never dowie –
Save when the ref. stude watchin there,
Was Andra Bowie!

Hei Cornet was, in 'forty-echt,
And won his Sash withoot a fecht,
Galloped The Wynd wi a' his micht,
Leading the fray.
A'body swat frae morn till nicht,
Yon "Shirt-sleeve Day!"

But now hei's bye his Nibbie- 'eer,
Wi bonnie wife and faimily dear,
Works hard to gether a bit gear,
Skilled at his trade,
Has a strang preference for beer
Owre lemonade!

There's men that chase the fox on nags,
Crawl Hielan' corries efter stags,
Rivin' their troosers into rags,
For sport, nae doot,
And some that guddle Tarras haggs
For braw bull-troot.

There's some that speel up rocky faces,
Scrievin their hides in nameless places –
To mei, the hail o' them's heid-cases,
But that's their ploy,
If they've a mind to burst their braces,
Aa wush them joy.

Some'll wade, chitterin, 'bune their kneis,
Leatherin Esk wi saumon-fleis,
Some pech wi beagles owre the leys,
And think it pleesant –
But Aa ken only yin clim's treis
To catch a pheasant!

(for Edgar Morrison – Langholm Cornet 1948)

HERMITAGE

Auld Warlock Hermitage
There on the haugh,
Sits square on his hurdies
And gies a bit lauch.

Whut'rope and Sundhope
They ken the soond weel;
It's nae news to thaim
That he troks wi the deil.

The Nine-stanes, his kimmers,
Can snirk at his game,
But Cauldcleuch and Gritmuir
Think black-burnan shame –

For doon i the dungeons
Gleg Reid-cap still lurks,
In plain disregaird
For the Office o Works!

THE HERNSEUGH

The hernseugh fisht the swawin' pule
In blew days and grey,
And niver cam' a thing ava
To gliff the lad away.

Whiles hei saw a herlin soom,
And whiles killt a troot –
Niver o' his awnership
Had hei a meenit's doot;

Till ae day a sharrybang
Cam' doon the lang brae,
And niver was the hernseugh
Seen thrae that day.

Back cam' the soople spugs
And ate the auld breid,
But puir lang-craigit hernseugh
Had mair pride than greed.

THE LEAVES

Come in, November, and match my mood,
Wi' the band braying frae the park
On Remembrance Sunday, wi the damp
Invadin' everywhere the agein' banes
O' the year, stiffenin' the mairchin' step
O' medalled veterans.

There is nae resurrection o' the leaves
That birl slowly doon.
Only the poppies are immune
Wiry and stiff in the dark lapels.
The bugler blaws his best,
But the Last Post is date-styled already
By the remorseless years.

The padre mouths the words,
And a deid leaf settles on his shooder
Like a chip, garrin' his words
Soond half-defiant, less than half believed
By the silent crood.
Shiftin frae fit to fit in the mush o leaves:
The year's brood.
"I am the resurrection and the leaf"
And there is nae leaf,
Till the arrogant spears, cruel and shairp,
Bristle the armout of another spring.

LAN' – WARD BRED

I canna schule mysel' to fit
Wi tounsmen, drawn sae keen the bricht
Upon each other's avarice;

Nor can I thole their snack-bar wit,
Their bowlers and their brilliantine:
Owre slow am I to bear a pairt.

For I was lan' –ward bred, and lang
For thick-broon at brig-ends, and speech
As blunt's the erse-brod o' a cairt.

THE DEAN

They're dirty craws that dwall i' the Dean,
The coorsest craws that ever war seen;
Like thieves they come, wi' fly side-hoppin's
And nane considerate o' their droppin's.

Dirty white-wesh, deid-rot treis,
Baked-bean tins and mawky fleis,
A stinkin' midden, a scartin' hen –
There's sma' choice there 'tween craws and men.

GOLDFINCH

The cage-bird, auld Gowdie,
Comes whurrin' and friskin',
Lichts on my shooder
And nibbles my lug.

Strange, but hert-reachin',
Be'in ta'en for a mug
By an unce o warm ooder
Wi a wide-aware e'e . .

I'm nae Franciscan:
He does the preachin
Wi sma frail chirls
I guess at to be
Some kind o craiter-to-craiter
Civility.

THE MUNE

THE MUNE IS BUT A RICKLE O' STANE –
I maun gang oot, I maun gang oot,
HER WUNDS THEY NIDDER TILL THE BANE –
The mune she shines sae bricht,
Till a' the yirth is marlt wi'
The grymins o' her licht.

SHE'S BUT THE SHOOTIN' – CHEESE O' MAN –
I maun gang oot, I maun gang oot,
GIEN TO THE STERNS WHEN LIFE BEGAN –
The mune she shines sae clear,
An' a' the yirth aneth her look
Lies dappled like a deer.

O I AM YOUNG, OUR BRIDE-BED'S WARM –
I maun gang oot, I maun gang oot,
I FEAR HER LILITH-LOOK, HER HARM –
The mune she shines sae bricht,
Till a' the yirth aneth her een
Is fu' o' loppert licht.

. . . .

Shootin-cheese . . . a cheese presented to the gossips by the father, when a child is born.
(Roxburghshire Word-Book)

COMMON-RIDING TOAST

(1970 Common-Riding Dinner, Cornet Ronald K. Gibson)

Aa whiles think that life in this grey auld toon o' Hawick
Micht weel be compared to a river . . . ,
And what better river than oor ain Te'iot itsel' . . .
Rinnin canny and clear for the maist pairt;
Whiles risin' in a freshet o New 'Eer snaw;
Whiles low and weariet-like in times o drouth or dearth;
Whiles wi a touch o temper, efter a thunner-plump
Away up thonder abune the Wusp . . . at Westminster . . .
Whiles rinnin drumly wi contention o politics
As callants and candidates rive divots frae opposite banks
And daub them dourly at yin another . . .!

But there's yin time o the 'eer when the river o life
In Hawick swalls suddenly until a rip-tide
And rins bank and brae, cairryin a'thing afore it . . .
Roarin bye . . . horses and hobby-horses . . . shuggy-boats . . .
And stucca-dolls and coconut-shies and drums and fifes . . .
And auld freends, and lang-lost neebors, and bairns
Hauf-mad wi the pleesure o'd . . .
And, in auld times, yon raw o somnolent stocking-makers,
Blissfu', sleepin't a' off, aneth the muckle trei
That stude sae lang at the fit o the Nipknowes,
Gey and handy for thon spring o caller waitter
To slocken the stoorie road to fresh tents
          and pint-pots new . . .
Or, strakkit wi a stound o conscience, to face
A vinegar wife owre a preen-cushion
          dish o potted herring . . .

Aye . . . the Common Riding flude's in full spate . . .
Risin, here, ebbin a bit, there . . . ebbin for the day
Frae Hawick Muir, wi its guaird o hills doverin
Into a dappled sleep . . . ebbin to leave a jettison
O' threi-to-yin-bar-yin bookies' tickets,
Orange-peel, horse-shairn, and shipwrecked bottles
Full o naething but broken
          pledges and impossible promises . . .
Risin, even now, in the Haugh, as the Yin-airmed Bandits
Clash and clatter and gobble
          doon the last undecimal coppers
Wi neither shame nor signs o indigestion . . . !
Full flude . . .
The saturnalia in full swing and full sang . . .

And as aa try to soom oot to the wild and willowed shore
To look at it, and attempt to propose its guid health,
Aa'm like to foonder beneath a cargo o maimories . . .
Maimories, and devotions, and comparisons . . . for this
Is the first o the ancient private tribal festivals,
And gaun, as usual, like a kirn-milk mairket!
<u>Threi</u> ancient private tribal festivals within 35 miles . . .
The threi aa ken best . . . Hawick, Selkirk and Langholm . . .
(The order's juist chronological, and nae offence to the rest.)
They're a' Common Ridings . . . twae of them wi Cornets,
Yin wi a Standard Bearer . . . twae wi nae official Lass,
But wi a routh o lasses welcome to bob and scrammle
Alang wi the lave . . . A' within 35 miles o Borderland . . .
A' wi their ain quirks and sacred ceremonies
That have "aye been" . . .
                . . . and naebody kens
Ony o them, that hasna kent them
Since he was a bairn . . . born and bred till't,
Wi a Common Riding in the verra blude-stream . . .
Burley-men and halberdiers, and "Drums i' the Walligate
Pipes i the air . . . Come and hear the Cryin o The Fair . . ."
And Tibbie Tamson and St. Leonards, and Whita Well,
And the Three Brethern, and the Ca' Knowe . . .

And so, we salute, and we a' welcome a' veesitors
At ilka Festival . . . welcome them as bidden
Or unbidden guests . . .And Everybody allows
The fundamental misfortune o the Tother
In no' bein' born till't . . . and therefore and for ever
Nae mair . . . and nae <u>less</u> than the welcome stranger
Within the yetts . . .
Everybody's Common Riding's the Best Common riding . . .
As Everybody kens . . . and lang may they flourish
Wi their ain tribal ploys and ceremony and sang . . .
A' within 35 miles . . . and a' begun wi the yin object . . .
To watch and guaird their Common Land.

But there's a strange wund blawin aboot the Borderland . . .
A wund o Change . . . wi a queer Regional sough . . .
And aa hed a cheese-supper dream the tother nicht
That some day we'll feenish wi a Regional Common Riding . . .
Located in some centralised rationalised place this side o Stow,
Wi' a' the sangs and ceremonies and flags and flutes and pipes
And drums and fifes and quirks and whurly-whas
Fed intil a computer that'll gang "ga-doing, ga-doing"

And come oot wi an answer frae St Andrew's hoose
Designed, wi Regional Approval to embody the best
Regional Features o a' the Regional Festivals . . .
. . . And God help the Liaison Committee . . . ! They'll need
Murrayfield to meet in . . . Wallace the Bruce for Convener . . .
And auld Solomon himsel' as Chairman . . . !

But that was a nichtmare . . . And aa've stude
Lang enough here, i' the shallows
        wi the baggies nibbling ma taes,
. . . The Common Riding flude gang
        whurlin and whummlin on . . .
Til its destination in the sei o history . . .

But no' juist yet, awhile . . .
For already, the lasses are primpin at their keekin-glesses,
Getting buskit for the Ball. And the auld Moat,
That's seen hunders o Common Ridings,
Sits hotchin up thonder like an ancient dowager,
Waitin for daylicht and her dancin Callants . . .

. . . And the raw o somnolent stocking-makers
Have lang been gethered to their hindmaist sleep,
And the muckle Nipknowes trei chippit doon . . .

But we're a' stocking-makers' bairns and grand-bairns,
And the second Cornet o my life-time is here
Among us a', and hale and herty . . . and lang may he be! . . .
Cornet, when the Common Riding rose again
Like a phoenix frae the holocaust o the First War . . .
A Cornet, symbolic o mony a lang-lost callant
In fremmit fields, that micht have carried the Flag . . .
And so the Common Riding rose again . . .
        twice in my time . . .
Rose in glory . . . and in glory, lang may it gang on . . .
Yince an affair o stern duty; but now an affair o the hert . . .
And there's owre little hert, nowadays, mair's the peety . . .
For, as a wice and wayward man yince said:
"The hert's aye the pairt, aye, that makes us richt or wrang."

Lang may the Common Riding leeve in the herts
O' every leal Teri . . . stirrin to the auld sangs . . .
"The kindly customs, words and deeds . . ."
And the auld Flag that's borne wi sic pride
By a Hawick Callant, on each Common Riding Morn . . . . !

DERK WI' RAIN

The clouds sail slow doon Teviotdale
Owre every hope and grain,
The road and river wanly glint
And the hills are derk wi' rain.

The wund raves through the scruntit thorn
And sheep for bield are fain,
The parks are ribbed wi' meltin' snaw
And the hills are derk wi' rain.

The snawdrops may in Branxholme woods
Nod promised spring again,
For earth has certainty to ease
Her yearly childing pain.

But I'll face to the hills this day,
The hills sae derk wi' rain,
Nor easy valley omens seek –
While bairns sterve deid in Spain.

1936

THE JOURAL-I-JOO

The jougals yowl't at the jooral-i-joo
Whaniver hei stert' tae play;
A shilpit scurryvaig hei was,
And shuttle-gobbit tae,
As hei bruisslt and whewed the bullet-shells,
And bang't the drum away.

Pretensic fowk gaed primpin' by,
Snirkin' at sic a din,
Only the jougals hunkert roond,
Enjoyment seemed tae fin' –
Or war the critters yowlin' at
The plicht their god was in?

. . . .

Jougals . . . . . . .dogs
Jooral-i-joo . . . a one-man-band
Pretensic . . . . .pretentious
Scurryvaig . . . .a ragged vagrant
(Roxburghshire Word-Book)

THE BACCA-BLAW

(with acknowledgements to Hugh MacDiarmid)

Ae nicht last week, meeting Jock Trummle,
He speired yon needfu thing
A cigarette, wi its hertenin licht,
Solace to bring,
An' I wonder at his wild look o greed
Afore I gied!

But there's nae reek i Jock Trummle's hoose
This nicht – an' nane i mine,
An' I've wantit to gie his jaw a dicht
Ever sin' syne,
For hevan seen the papers noo, I ken
What he kent then!

“SCAB”

(Wild Parsley)

Up the manse glebe
Where the brae bends sweet,
Was sic a fraith o’ scab
As ca’d halt to my feet.

Fient anither floo’er there,
Naething mair, nor less,
Than the swing o’ the road
Throwe the lang swayin’ gress

And bonny scab, bairn-high,
Whiter than whey,
On a girny simmer’s day
Wi’ a tear in its ei.

Hawick News, July 4th 1975

WAR POETRY

EAST ANGLIA – 1940 – 1941

(Honington, 9 Squadron – Wellingtons.)

This is nae place for a Border man to gaun aboot.
Niver a brae to pech up ower
Niver a view. . . .

The wind is too much with us, late and soon,
Blasting and roaring it lays waste our powers:
Mocking our efforts when there is no moon
To cover main-planes in the midnight hours.
From these October days until next June
We must endure its hate, the slashing showers –
Arrows of rain, and buckshot hail – its tune
Of shrieking devilment. While mankind cowers
And cares for thatch and latch in this flat land.

In the quiet cold of the barrack room,
In this ripe and stagey season
Melancholy is borne on every wind
That pipes in the ear and points
At all the dowager pomp of trees:
Stealing up with mock reverence,
Wooing them till they sigh,
Requiring calm to maintain precarious dignity,
Then snarling, tweaks their cloaks
And is off and away. A treacherous time
When from the inside of the window shows
An innocent snail-gallop of scalloped clouds
Strung across the sky as in summer days.
But going out-doors the air is edged, and the wind
An importunate demon.

IN NOVEMBER

Along the water-meadows
Crop-headed willows stand,
A humble regimented crowd, torches in hand,
Watching their dead borne slowly past,
Slain by this tyrant season.

In lanes the leaves' splayed fingers
Catch fallen urchin fruit
Winking from split pith like a colonel's boot:
Glinting basilisk-eyed when the moon
Leers over lip of cloud.

And over stubbled acres
Moves an uneasy air,
A wind from outer dark, swinging pair by pair
The gape-mouth bells in the flinty tower
That tongue no more for God.

THE SHEDDIN'

Yin day Aa was sittin' i' the efternune sun
The larks i' the lift were singin'
An emmet ran up a blade o' gress
And beis thrae the clover were hingin'.

A' roon' aboot stude the muckle black birds,
Quiet and glutted wi' bellys-fi daith,
Ready to roar away in the gloaming
Wi' gallus young lads that think lichtly o' scaith.

There wasna a soond, till sudden there sterted
A beh-in' and meh-in' thrae miles away
That rose and fell and rose and died down
And a'body swithered and thocht "What's adae?"

But mony's the time aa've heard sic-like cryin'
Thrae yowes i' the stells in the warm July days –
Sleekit collies rinnin', hirds whusslin' and yellin'
And lood the lamentin' bi haughs and bi braes.

And ma hert was seek for the days that are gane,
Mebbe gane for a' time, as youth driffles by,
And a lad wi' a fishin' wand wanders nae mair
Bi the burns o' the muirland where lanely whaups cry.

And sae, as the cryin' gangs up i' the Border
Bi Tarras and Hermitage, Ettrick and Yill,
There's sheddin' o' sheep that forget sune their hame-steed
An' sheddin' o' men whae's herts never will.

The desolate crying of sheep fills every glen and cleuch at this time o eer, says Hab. The deep bleating of bereft mothers and the high, lost, keening of orphaned lambs is woven into the very fabric of our landscape, and the best of our songs voice their desolation.

LEAVE IN MARCH

Snowdrifts, leprous and ashamed, lurking behind
Dykes or crouched in hollows . . .
Crocuses, bright as blown flame, cool-white, mauve-veined;
Lupin leaves like tiny green hands.
Blue smoke of garden fires drifting across the hazy
Pale shafts of sunlicht . . .
Soil, crumbly and rich brown, paling to thin dust
in the sun . . .
A worm, jewelled with sunlight, butting and retracting
after being turned up by the spade.
Crows, brittle and silky-lustrous as charcoal, croaking,
twig-carrying . . .
Bees drunk with the pale sweet wine of the spring sun.

HANGARS

The wind in the dark and rain
Likes not these raw square buildings:
They have no moulded frailty
Like plaster and thatch, rattling latch
Of cottages that cower like creatures of the field
Streamlining themselves to slipstream fury.

Square, concrete and steel, they stand
And the wind that has ripped and shattered
Endless panzer billows cannot shake them.
It comes beating with great fists, straining,
Panting like thwarted giant,
But they stand, rock-fast and unmoved.

But the wind will have them in the end:
Some day science will blow them apart
That built them, for they will be no more use
To men. The wind will have its way
With them, but cottages will be there:
Reed of thatch once reed of river loses no cunning,
The willow defers, grass repeats sea,
And over the mangled jangle of old iron,
The wet-stained crumble of concrete,
Wind will whip, snarl, blast with rain
in final triumph. That labourer
Hooded in wet sacks, driving the plodding cart
Knows this already, as surely as spring sowing.

ENGLISH

PENSIONER'S ELECTION

Long grown old in hungry usage
To the rationed fags, the week-end pint,
The state-occasional dram
He sits before the life-enhancing box
Listening to the fat-jowled bores
Flogging their nonsense, knowing
It but his cross on paper
That really matters. He carries
The cross of a life's work
With no security and scant comfort!
Has the guilt he must swallow
With his pint that should have been
A loaf of bread. To work
A life should be enough
Without gut-worry, and spent muscles
Dragging at the hammered nails
Of poverty. But, for Joe, from the start,
It was never on.

GO WALK-ABOUT

The vulnerable ones: they
Cannot cope with life
Without a shell
To get by.

Some curl-up in their private
Heaven or hell
Go underground.
Others grow legs, and get around.

The legs presume a higher stage
Of evolution:
If that means anything to you,
Brother, shall we, perhaps,
Take a tentative step?

We might as well
Give it a try.

SEARCH

Beat no frenzied frail hands
On the sere pane that will not yield.
Strike no chord; for they have
All been struck.

Search in vain all the octaves'
Compass; ichor-thin treble
And the curdled thrum of bass,
But it is no use. It is in vain.

You must seek some quarter-tone,
Some sixteenth-tone that will
Slice air like an edged knife;
Cleave the brain, shatter the pane

So that the glass explodes away
In powder, and you can
Look forth and lock fingers
With the earth your lover.

VERDICT OF HISTORY

His path was steep, he had no guide,
Yet gallantly he groped a way;
With bleeding fingers tried
Sheer cliffs on either side.

But perched upon a later day,
The easy vantage-point of fools,
Pedantic monkeys say
He fell between two stools.

With greater loss they'll pass
Beneath Time's concave glass.

THE BEECH

All summer long, I heard the roar
Of surf that never reached a shore;
And now upon the faded turf
Is tawny shore, no sounding surf.

She that was niggard of her green
When beggar winds the branches rolled,
By frost and slow decay has been
Made spendthrift of her lovely gold.

Pity her not, though she makes play
With bony hands – 'tis mock dismay;
For soon her mining roots will send
Tight-fisted copper dividend.

This happy pauper needs but bide
The certain turning of the tide.

SOME DAY

Some day I will buy
A great amplifier and a great
Transcription turntable and a
Great cartridge with an elliptical
Diamond stylus
And play it all through somebody's
Great bass-drivers and tweeters
And Christ-knows what'.

But none of it will sound like
Beecham on my old old set
Playing Berlioz before
Most of you were born:
Beecham. T. Brain. D.
On horn.
You cannot reckon or conjure
Magic into the diabil:
It just happens. Harty or Beecham.
Stereo. Cheerio. Merry Hell.

MAY NIGHT

The blackbirds are shouting at each other
In the dusk, in the rain
Of late spring. Is it a song: a rejoicing
in life? Or, as some maintain,
Merely laying loud claim
To terrain?

I do not know. Maybe all song
Is a claiming of something or other.
Or Compensation, Form 102, for regret.
Perhaps some day blackbirds will evolve
An art-form for anguish,
But it will take a long, long time.

Meanwhile, in the days that are left to me,
I will settle for "Die Mainacht" of Brahms.

SNOW

Snow I both hate and fear:
Not the face-slapping wet flakes
That are merely sliced Christmas cards
In a dank Wenceslas motorcade,

But the blinding grandlar ground-twirling,
Driving, vertically-spinning spume
That invades the snarling dark:
Dracula in the old old film,
But faceless – never coagulating into the stare,
And the goulish tiger-teeth.

I sense it as a crazed racial memory – beyond
Blue-faced, bath-longing legionaries on The Wall –
Beyond huddled stinking pelts of the Stone Age –
To men who knew these howling dervishes
Dancing death for the defenceless;
Knew the mad keening, before words and history,
Through millimetre-slow ice-capped millenia.

TO THE OBOE

Yours is an earthless, rare delight
Pure as the searching wind
High snowfields tracing in the lean moon's light
Reed with the bitter rind.

Weirdly astringently you cleave
The tender, misted strings,
Patterns of earth's loveliness they weave
But your song has wings.

Lost causes with your sister flute
Passionately you plead
Forlornly singing when all else is mute
O plaintive lyric reed.

Surely some elf-locked wandering god
In the green age of spring
Made all the gay flowered wilderness he trod
Silent to hear you sing.

And wild with wonder at your birth
All ruder speech forsook
And wandered far across the blue-hilled earth
Till by a snow-fed brook,

He died. But still his poet's heart
In you, bewitched, must dwell
To wake whene'er the piper with his art
Can cast the ancient spell.

Is this the secret of your note
Strangely nostalgic, pure,
Whose beauty takes us sudden by the throat?
We wonder, still unsure

And mockingly your song goes on;
We still must hear
And wonder till frail sense is gone
Till dulled and dead our ear.

1951

ILL WIND

Ill wind, indeed, to blow no good:
When foresters cut down the wood
That climbed the hillside gallantly,
I stopped and cursed them where I stood.

Of all that laughing company,
They left one shivering-naked tree,
The livid ashes of their fires,
And the white stumps of surgery.

Ill wind, indeed, to blow no good:
When next I passed that one-time wood,
So thick were foxgloves' rosy spires
I stopped and marvelled where I stood;

For men had left a rag forlorn
To temper where they'd rudely shorn,
But earth had given the wounded wood
A cloak that put them all to scorn.

1936

RIPENESS IS ALL

Would that I, like Rembrandt
In old age, could look in a mirror
And see, not myself,
But a completely objective piece
Of human flesh, lighted and shaded
Weathered and tide-beaten
By sixty decades:

Observe the battered face,
The wrinkles, the bottle-nose;
Observe the serene maturity
That could see and accept
All these things and set them out
With consummate skill in paint;

Observe the eyes, old and experienced,
Which, even looking in a mirror
See, and with faultless integrity
Record, for all time – to heartbreak –
The ageless, ruthless, majesty of art.

THIRD PROGRAMME

14 Rosebank Road, Hawick - October 29, 1946

Sir, - Persistent failure to get the Third Programme is my excuse for the following:-
LAMENT FOR THE THIRD PROGRAMME
(Quhen He Wes Sek of Twiddland Diallis)

I that in heill wes, and gladnes,
Am troublit now with gret madness
And rageand at the B.B.C
514. 203.

On 391 I get the Newis
On 261 there's Swing and Blewis –
Bot sik-lik thingis are nocht for me.
514. 203.

Weiks syne I tried for, first of aw,
"Don Juan in Hell" by Bernard Schaw –
As far as thair I bad thaim be.
514. 203.

Last nicht I made a bid richt bold
To hear "Tristan and his Isold"
Ane kitlin-mew micht louder be.
514. 203.

This nicht I have been sair strivand
To hear som sangis by Dowland,
Allace! I wes up ane gumme-tre!
514. 203.

"Where does the uttered music go?"
You may search me. I do nocht kno –
Performit Wodensday it will be.
514. 203.

To see thingis in "The Radio Times"
And hear thaim nocht, incites to crimes –
Like writeand Middle-Scots Phonie.
514. 203.

Sen for the quid remeid is none
Best is that we for bed dispone –
Promisit –lang-leevit gif we be –
514. 203.

I am &c. David Hill

'Scotsman' 1/11/46

THEATRICAL GENERALISATION

'Neath many an actor's ego
There lurks a secret ham,
A thund'rous black-browed Iago
As rich as damson jam

He longs to roar like Kemble
And every wither wring,
But doomed to shrug and mumble,
His gestures tied with string,

His thwarted histrionics,
Condemned to off-stage life,
Are drowned in gin-and-tonics
Or battles with his wife

1947

WITHY-BASKET

In the end, all he cared about was words.

The idea, its expression in rough form, and,
sometimes the lyric lift. But finally it was
always the words: the withy-basket, peeled of
bark and woven into some kind of shape.
The withy-basket sometimes peeled beyond the
bark to reveal a sliced, clean, pith of
unexpected truth. This was the withy-basket
that contained my heart and harns. Without it
I could not have lived, and I have no care who
will ever read or rate its merit.
It has earned me nothing, but that is not without
precedent. I have seen fools grow fat on
fatuity and the sweat of other men.
All I have ever done is to make withy-baskets of
words: unfashionable and crude to some ears, but
always diligently wrought in the hope that somewhere
there was somebody who would say
"I am glad, I am sure, because I remember
it was so."

SCOTS

LAST THOCHTS O' A HAGGIS

(glow'rin' a' roond, while bein' "addressed" at a Burns Supper)

"Fair fa' ma honest, sonsie face!" –
Look at your ain – a dem'd disgrace!
A' stannin', droolin', at your place,
Like hauf-sterved muggers:
Sma' credit to the human race,
Ye hungry buggers!

I'll tak' my aith, ye've hed nae tei,
So's ye could fill your wames wi' mei
And my puir neebors, makin' threi:
Painch, neeps and spuds –
And if wi' that ye dinna 'grei,
Ye're tellin' whuds!

It's no' sae much juist bein' ett'n –
Tho' sic a trial I'm no' forgettin' –
But, if the form's ocht like the bettin',
There's waur things still:
It's droonin tae, that sets mei frettin',
In drams and yill.

Each 'eer, as Januar' – end returns,
Ilk yowe and stirkie waefu' murns,
"They'll hae oor puddens oot by turns –
"We'll get oor paiks!
"A' owre-the-heid o' Rabbie Burns,
"Yon king o' raiks."

So…. I'm weel-weshed, then stapped wi' ingin,
And yits and liver, lites, and a' thing,
Tormentit ticht wi' steeks an' stringin',
Syne jagged wi' preens!
Then boiled until wi' sweit I'm wringin' –
For yowe – ye fiends !

A-weel – the piper waits to blaw,
Ye wait there, smirkin', raw on raw –
May ye a' chowk, and deid doon-fa'! –
Jock! Tam! or Wullie …..
In vain, upon the Lord I ca' …..
Here comes the gully

29/1/69

REMEMBRANCE

"O leaves that on the road
Your coinage spread,
You go not all unmourned
For beauty dead;

"We who know many springs
Yet know but one….."

So wrote I, in glib youth,
And left undone.

Now, in an aulder tongue,
My middle years
Bring leaf-fa thochts owre stark
For ony tears:

Yon gowd o' Martinmas
Cleeds timely daith.
I mind o' braw Whutson lads:
Green was their graith.

HOGMANAY, 1954

(Part of a radio BBC New Year Broadcast at New Year)

This yin nicht, o a' the nichts i' the year,
Be it mirk or munelicht or mirry wi' jigging stars,
In his bothy, Auld Time keeps open hoose, like a' guid men.

The World, The Flesh, and the Deil are colloguin' there,
As the Auld Year patiently stands to thole his assize.
"Bad," says The World – "men compete
To blaw muckle holes in ma biggin."
"Guid," says The Flesh – "men speiled to the tap o' your riggin."
"Dyach!" says The Deil. Time nickers and says nocht;
The sands in his gless dwine doon.

The kimmers Faith and Hope gledge oot o the lamp-lit door
Into the wundy derk o Eternity –
And as they rax to bring ben the unkennt bairn,
It's Charity, alane, hears the quiet clink o the sneck
As the Auld Year takes the road.

A Guid New Year.

ROWAN

Bousie wi flourish,
My rowan beams
Like a drucken bride . . . . .

Ach, ye're no' foolin me,
Ye brazent hag,
Wi your wrunkled hide;

I've been to your waddins
Owre often afore,
At Whussan-tide.

But she juist heezed her coats
And cried Bowff,
Ye toornie auld' man! –
So ye'll ken I've got scarlet
And gowd for gaun-away claes:
Ye should bide, if ye can.

“THE PAINS”

Yin comprehensive tairm
Covers them a’ –
Birth pangs, rheumatics
And deid-thraw!

1976.

LUSUS NATURAE

(Comment to 'The Scotsman', 25th October 1952, on a report of a thrush with two heads in a Westmorland gairden)

There's a twae-heidit mavis in Westmorland
That sings at the brek o day;
While the yin heid yokes on the airly worm
The tother chants its lay.

Syne, when their stammack's satisfied,
The twae heids cry, "Weel met!"
And tunin their twaefauld thrapple up,
Unite in a braw duet.

The bird-watchin man i the berry-buss
Sweirs at the jags and grunts,
And polishes up his binoculars
For fear they hae taen the strunts;

And a' the gibs i the neeborhood
Girn in a wild dismay –
But little the mavis fashes its heids:
Fower een are better than twae!

AIBERDEEN STATUARY

Rauchle gulls daily re-anoint
Enthroned King Edward

Wha took owre mony
Queyns bedward.

Whiles, at The Daisy and The Bard,
They tak their spite –
But it's a gey coorse maa daur fyle
Wallace, wight.

"A LITTLE FISH?"

When, after the first op.
I had to be starved for days
On sips of water, occasionally
Iced, according to the whim
Or busyness of night-staff,

I got tea one morning, and
Was one up on water.
Then, at dinner-time
Sister said – "Like a little fish?"
I took the plate and ate,
With tears on my face
Like a hungered
Dog at a dish. And as I ate
I heard old old singing
Of a paraphrase in voices
Now eternally dumb
Of an old Hebrew psalm
To the tune "Kilmarnock" –

"Come let us to the Lord our God
"With contrite hearts return,
"Our God is gracious nor will leave
"The desolate to mourn."

Then, licking my chops,
I thought that the
Auld Testament had muckle mense:
No immortality patter –
Just present thankfulness
For a little fish, to something
Or somebody beyond commonsense.

UNTITLED

I come from Flower Shows
Wi primpin roses oa a' shades
And gaudy gulled dahlias
To walk up the waterside
And see them battlin through concrete
Harebells frailer – thin
Than a robin's leg
And twice as teuch.

"<u>BIRD-SONG AT EVENTIDE</u>."

(Othello)

The Blackie's on
His up-stage brainch
The auld egg opera
Begins.

His sagg's a groundel
O' auld regrets –
While doon in thon hedge
The spugs are chirlin
Aboot spring-cleaned sins.

A.7

In the November night
There is only the lechery
Of the wind, raping the last
Resisting trees,

The black road
The bleached pavements
And the sad susurrus
Of retreating tyres.

UNTITLED

Scotland was a modern Athens
Aye, it lived on the backs of slaves
And starved or drove to Bedlam
Its bards intil their graves.

RISE, CARLINE, RISE

The carle rade tae Aberdeen
To buy white breid
But lang or he cam back again
The carline she was deid.
Sae he up wi his muckle stick
An' gied her ower the heid,
Cryin, "Rise, carline, rise,
An' eat white breid."

LAST TRUMP

What were your arles, Tam:
What did ye hain
Efter a life's work
For a maister's gain?

"I was a dyke-back gett:
A bondager's wean,
Wi' never ocht but the bothy-cat
To ca my ain."

"I can mind how <u>he</u> striddled
At the wunda-pane
Watchin' me shaw his neeps
I' the dirlin' rain."

"Ye wrocht gey sair, Tam:
Was't a' in vain . . .?
"Weel, the pairish yirds <u>my</u> kind
Thegither, gey plain – "

"But I'll up throwe thir divots
Afore <u>him</u>: massy, his lane,
Ablow thon lee'in' hunderwechts
O' marble stane!"

"He'll scrauch: Tam! Help!
What the deil are ye dae'in?
Quick! Gie's a hand to wun-oot! . . . .
But he'll get nane."

THE BATH OF SATURN

When the wund blaws canny
I' the kindly sooth,
Wi' the barest hint
O' heather in her mooth:

When yalla-girdit beis
Gar yin turn and look
To see whae's conversin' –
Jamie has a douk.

He scrubs his wrinkled hide
Wi' a fresh green sod,
Then owre the heid and oot
As shairp as a tod:

But naebody's seen him
In the caller pule,
First crottled wi' soil,
Then white – the auld fule!

Then he staps his pipe
Wi' bacca rank,
And trots till he's dry
Alang the bank,

Wi' a gledge at the sky
As the cutty reeks,
A demm at a thistle
And on wi' his breeks.

Jamie is a man
Can sweer gey broadly;
But aince an 'eer
He's next to godly.

AULD ROWAN

Auld rowan they have maimed
Wi surgery your brainches
Maimed mei, as weel.
Yet still your spreit sends forth
Green promises o life and leaf
So, sune, may some auld-farrant sap
Set my sangs frei,
To cheat the deil
O' the saul's desolation

1976.

DERKENIN'

The nicht's dreary,
The treis are steery
In a murnin wund,
And the lilacs are lockit ticht
I' their maidenhead;

But my auld hoor
O' a rowan, rangy
Wi life, gars spreid, lauchin still,
Her white-airmed charms
Abreid.

WHAT A PEETY!

The dirdums o' the wheezlebugs
Chunter the lee-lang day
And for a smarroch o' scowderdowps
My greasly hert is wae.

O that the gruntlebogs and wirrricows
Wadna addle my wuts
And the soreichspurtled slaisterbags
Wad gralloch my guts!

But the wail o' the snotter-gripe
Rises aye in my hert
Inhibiting since mair the Zeitgeist
Before I can get a stert.

And sae wi an ectoplasmic doppelgänger
I am doomed aye to warstle –
Unless mebbe it's a whustlecrowdie
Disguised as a thistle.

DELILAH

I made my hert a hedger's glove
Tae hain integrity,
Nor tae the sma' derk thorns o' love
A moment's thocht did gie;

Until a lass wi'r saft sweet words
Did wyle the glove in play,
And watch't the thorns drive deep as swords,
And laugh't – and gaed her way.

THE NON-COMPUTER

(The Haly Sanct Jock said: (1.V.1)
"In the Beginning was the Word . . .
And the Word was God" –
The trouble began
When the Numbers took over.

SPRING

What's wrong wi the world? –
Ilk lilac-spike, bronze hard
As a Valkyrie spear-heid
Suddenly softens, scents, transmutes
Intil a Rhine maiden!

What's wrong wi the world?
We expectit a hard wunter.
We hed mony haws – and nae snaws,
Nae yowdendrifts or snawplough drifts
Or ocht to girn aboot
But a pickle rain!

And now the chestnuts spreid braid fingers
Haudin candles
Til the Glory o Gode!
Sweir, and secretly surprised
For a' oor dour forebode,
We maun concede. It's Spring!

And we never even got
A dacent fa' o' snaw.
It's niver like the thing.
We dinna really gie in
Wi this kinna thing.
What ails the ice-cap?
Where's a' the snaw?

“LACRIMAE RERUM”

The blithe birds sing
This Aprile night,
And why they sing
Is nae my wyte,

But still their sang
Can bleer my een
For things that waur
Or micht hae been.

COUNTERPOINT

The mavis wales an up-stage brainch
The first act aria begins;
Linkin' owre the derkened yird
In caller whurly-whas and rins.

The sma-quilled buskers are happed in sleep,
Tam-tit's gien owre his cuddy-ca,
And robin' faulds his ragged pipes,
Reckons his arles and airts awa.

The young mune hauds her curtain bye
And stern and hoolet blink and stare,
And mony lang generations syne,
Cauldrife, I should hae lairnt to care

Nocht for yon rowel o whurly whas –
But still the singing clear and shair
Comes breistin abune the tides o nicht
To the cauldrife fule still stan'in there.

RENOIR'S "LA LOGE"

Thir roses, beekin
Full-breistit i the summer air
Hae the same leme o colour
As Mimi wore at her corsage
And braidit in her hair.

Ah, but the shell-petals
Drop, drifflin, frail doon
To their mortal lair.
But Renoir's roses.
And lovely frail Mimi,
Hersel a rose, though langsyne dust,
Will aye be there.

1975.

UNTITLED

Aa'm no' richt weel
Aa'm no' weel at a'
Wi my lugs preened back
'Tween the warlock and
The wa'.
Aa hae a sair skaith
That wunna skurl at a'.

UNTITLED

A set of dentures is decay:
Caries the first-maist sign o' daith.
Out, dock them and survey
Their grin: the plastic
Harbingers o' loss o' braith.

<u>ANE SONNET</u>

(for Anne Redpath)

Till A.R., quha passt his windaw ilk morning, armit with ane basket of wikkir to do battaill with the surlie marchands of the toune; bot gane a sennicht to Paisley, airly in Aprile.

Altho on buss and brier sweit foulis sing
And the dour grosert cleeds his thornis fell
With gentil grene, allace! the suith to tell
The matin sunlicht littel joy dois bring,
For in the blak-lummed wesst still lingering
Ye pass na by the windaw of my cell.
Demeter's bairn ane sessoun dwallt in Hell,
Bot aye retournit for retour of Spring,

So haist ye: in despair ilk crocus spills
Hir chaliced colour on the heedless grund,
The tossilit curran weips hir teirs of blude,
Nae primroisis will starre the wanhope wud,
Till serriet trumpets of the daffodils
Blaw Weill-com to Persephone unbund!

ATHEIST'S INJUNCTION

O saw your aits, and saw them wide,
And choose your sins yoursel'
But never on the Lord of Hosts
Get hunkert doon and yell

Though fraised ye be wi' terror-frost,
Or scorched wi' beauty's fire,
Keep aye your ain integrity,
Keep aye your saul entire.

Accept your aches, accept your paiks,
Reap your ain hairst o' follies;
It's men o' straw that jouk their law –
Jehovah's pet kirn-dollies.

. . . .

Kirn-dolly . . . . .a figure, bedecked with ribbons, made from the last handful of corn reaped on the harvest-field. (Roxburghshire Word-Book)

BARBER'S SHOP

A gallus auld tink,
I thocht wi the rest,
Whan ye said that at echty
A man's at his best!

But now it's your turn
To streek oot i the chair,
Happed a' in white
At the ceiling to stare;

And the barber completes
Wi a smother o graith
What we canna help seean:
The vestments o daith.

BACKYAIRD HENS

A' day, they raiked aboot the clatchy yaird,
Focht owre a hauf-drooned clocker, mobbed a craw,
Syne, crup thegither, hullerie,
Under the shelter-brod, watchin the cauld blashes
O' wet snaw wi bricht bead een,
Till Providence cam clatterin wi a pail,
And then steekit them safe i their din hoose.

Do they craik and churl and gossip, there,
I' the getherin derk, numberin the days
O' the sma noolt hen i the corner that never lays, …
Is their crack o' simmer ploys: story baths,
Hotchin and croonin in howes i the grund …
O' the frushness o green-meat … the coople awakeness
O' weel-faured worms …?

Craikin and churlin, till sleep blears their een,
And the bald eyelids shutter doon,
Stirrin, whiles, in nichtmares o auld hen-weirds –
Squatterin wi a thrawn neck,
Or the snap and crunch o a tod's teeth …

Croochin wi scaly claws lockit ticht to the spaik,
The lee-lang wunter nicht,
Till sweir daylicht.

DOUBTS

I think sometimes I'll leeve tae bless
The muckle dour self-consciousness
That bids me thraw my pen aside
An' let sic things as verses bide;

An' yet, the thing I cannae dae,
I maun explain a'thing away –
So sklim' high heaven, trinnle throw hell
Waitter and sit I ca' myself'!

NOVEMBER NICHTPIECE

The street's gain sudden blank,
The last char waddles by,
Hopn' the auld-yin's drunk
Himsel' hungert; no' a martyr.

That he has found the pie
She left him for supper-time,
And winna, for godsake, try
Auld argyments again;

Or (fou o regimental rum)
How he piped at Alamein,
And, hoin on detachment,
Played the wrang tune.

The auld indifferent mune
Takes a' things as they come;
The unpensioned single eye,
According til it's quarter,
Leers or stares blankly doon,
Oot o a blank sky.

THE SCOTTISH FIELD REPORT, April 1955

The Family Tree

Our traditions, of course, don't exist independently of each other: they are not separable into exact categories. And at the source of many of them there is one which is perhaps most difficult of all to analyse and define: the tradition of family life. What of the family tree today?

"The tree sprung from our soil bears many scars.
The stem is thrawn, but strong.
There are shameful stumps
Where bravery of branches should have spread.
The tree has bled – and healed – a hundred times,
The tree that is our Scottish race, our own,
What of the tree to-day? Does it throw abroad
Flower and fruit in free and airy growth
As once it did? Can it survive its singular self,
As the afforestation of uniformity creeps on,
Row upon standardised row, around the earth?
Does it dwine lank and lean,
Choked in the jungle-growth of alien weeds
That spawn across the continents in ways
That would have set our fathers muttering of warlocks –
Weeds that gain easy footing in an untilled soil
And creep to strangle-holds?
Let us look to our soil; keep the heuk and hoe
Rust-free and keen; husband with knowledge in our hands;
Keep what is ours strong and comely and clean.
It is necessary to cultivate our garden.
We have much to do; for there are things we can lose,
That, once lost, will leave us lost ourselves . . "

From David Hill's script "The Family Tree".

Easy to be sentimental about such things, too easy; to remember them not as they really happened but as if they were part of a story. But that may be because we live in a story; because we need a story to live in as much as we need air to breathe; or the way a bairn needs a story at night for reassurance that the world will go on through the darkness.

The word Scotland is the title of one of the stories we live in. Scotland the place has been discovered, explored, measured, and given its fixed designation at the centre of our map of the world. We live in the place, but we also live in the other Scotland, Scotland the story – the tradition, the inheritance, the promise for the future.

From the B.B.C. "Scottish Heritage" Series - The Family Tree

THE BONNY TREE
(the Rowan Tree)

(Prologue)

Sullen earth, sodden out-rig and in-field,
Rain-lashed and tree-less, stony, thin-stubbled
Beneath skies of scant mercy, breeding men
Of harsh beliefs in a punitive grim God,
Men with a sense of sin . . . .
 Men with a sense of kin,
Men bound together in run-rig commonty
And in the old unity of hall and hallan, tholing together
Poverty, and the heart-breaking caprice of elements.
Supping the same broath from slightly different bowls,
Chewing the everlasting saltness of the mart-beast
Or slorping the ever-abiding brose . . . . .
With an ear cocked for a change of airt . . . .
Praying for a miraculous pullulation in doo-cots,
Chewing the rangy sinews of cast hens . . . .
With an eye cocked for a change in the weather . . .
So that they might carry forth their stall-starved beasts
To gather strength from the first green blades of spring
To haul again the inept implements
That mauled the body of exhausted earth
For yet another puling puny harvest.

And yet the songs were born,
Whin-flowers of song, sparse and lovely gold,
To nod and spread on kindly airs of spring
Their spice and sprightliness . . .
Songs with a finger-snap of popping broom-pods.
Song and kindliness springing from earth-floored hovels.
The wind's song, keening through gable-gaps,
Stirring and swinging peat-reek. The jig of thatch-drip
In thaw, the flat-fish slap of freshening waves
On a boat's dance in dazzle and spray.
Song as cool and heart-catching as a sight of primroses
Peering through winter-blanched grass, song elusive as their scent
And the caller thin-spun line of lintie and lark . . . .

Song and kindliness and the sense of kin –
These have come down to us out of the dark.
The songs abide. Many old kindly ways have gone –
Suddenly, in blood and exile and harsh laws,
Slowly, as cossetted and courted earth increased its yield,
And black wealth came to those who owned its depths,
Slowly, in the cleavage of class into master and man,
Baronial tower and tenement, villa and miner's row . . .
And kinship, family, the old tree of Scotland,
Branched into sib and sept, cousinry and come o' wull:
The bonny tree.
What of its health?

1955

THE BONNY TREE

(Epilogue)

What we have for our own, is our tilth of tradition,
A soil hard-won for us in sweat and song,
In spare living, in dour devotion, in the blitheness of dancing,
By men who lie quiet now.

There was another soil, though under kindlier skies,
As sparse as ours, and yet surpassing all
In quality of yield. There are other, richer, soils
That bear a fatter harvest. We have our own.

The tree sprung from our soil bears many scars.
Its stem is thrawn, but strong. There are shameful stumps
Where bravery of branches should have spread.
The tree has bled – and healed – a hundred times,
The tree that is our Scottish race, our own.

What of the tree today? Does it throw abroad
Flower and fruit in free and airy growth
As once it did? Can it survive, its singular self,
As the afforestation of uniformity creeps on,
Row upon standardised row, around the earth?
Does it dwine lank and lean,
Choked in the jungle-growth of alien weeds
That spawn across the continents in ways
That would have set our fathers muttering of warlocks –
Weeds that gain easy footing in an untilled soil
And creep to strangle-holds?

Let us look to our soil; keep the heuk and hoe
Rust-free and keen; husband with knowledge in our hands;
Keep what is ours strong and comely and clean.
It is necessary to cultivate our garden.
We have much to do; for there are things we can lose,
That, once lost, will leave us lost ourselves . . . .
Rootless . . . . and lost. Let us be of a guid hert.
Let us cultivate our garden – our own garden – worthily.
Let us do that, and fear the less for our tree.

CHUCKS-MEI!

"CHUCKS-MEI!"

A choice of Pleasures, People and Places

By David Hill

(Read to Hawick Archaeological Society, 19th February, 1957)

"CHUCKS-MEI" was once quite a common expression in the Hawick district. I've heard my father use it, quite often; it's in the Roxburghshire Word Book; and a variant of it, "Chaps-mei," is still known in the Muckle Toon o' the Langholm.

Just imagine a wheen bairns with their noses up against a toy-shop window, choosing what they would like best. In my boyhood, it would have been, "Chucks-mei yon glessy bools!" Or "Chucks-mei yon bull-bater top." And a little lassie might have said, "Chucks-mei yon dolly's pram."

I head that there's a modern equivalent – "Bags-I." Slightly better grammar, maybe, but I don't fancy it much. However, I suppose the modern version would go something like this: "Bags-I that jet-bomber" or "Bags-I that space-suit." But, mind you, I still think the little lassie would say "Bags-I that dolly's pram," proving yet again that it's no' the weemen-folk that's flichty! It's the men wi' their trips to the mune! The lassies have their feet firm on the grund, beside their prams . . . .

Well, the title is "Chucks-mei" – which is guid braid Scots. The subtitle, "a choice of pleasures, people and places," is English; which shows that, while I couldn't resist using a good old Scots phrase, I had to go on to explain it in English. A state of affairs I'd like to enlarge on for a few minutes, as it has a bearing on the mixter-maxter of language in which this paper is written.

In the old days of Border strife, there was a tract of country between Sark in Scotland and Longtown in England, called the Debateable Land; a pleasant name with a flavour of John Bunyan, as well as of the wild gentry of the riding ballads. And the point about the Debateable Land is that it was sometimes Scots, sometimes English, and sometimes, I suppose, a bit of both.

Now it seems to me that most Scotsmen are, to some extent, dwellers in a Debateable Land of language. To the majority of us, Scots is the tongue we learned at our mothers' knee. The "kail" of our youth may become the "vegetable soup" of our middle-age (and be the wersher for it!) but it was kail we tasted first. Yet our education is conducted almost entirely in English, and we continue afterwards, to read, mainly in English, and to listen – to radio, films, and the result is that for most of us, Scots is the language of feeling, of emotion; and English the language of thinking. The classic example is Robert Burns, who wrote coolly and reasonably in English, in his letters, but who turned to Scots when emotion and intuition fused into great poetry.

In the lives of many folk, this language difficulty never arises. But to others, it can be quite a problem. There are the people, for instance, who decide, very early, that their native tongue is a hindrance; that even a Scots *accent* is a patched homespun coat which they cannot afford to be seen wearing on the rungs of their chosen ladder. But it is the writer who comes up against this language dilemma in its most perplexing form. There have been several ways of dealing with it. Hugh Macdiarmid – born on the edge of the real Debateable Land – tried heroically to re-create a Scottish language and to write in nothing else. William Souter, and others, did fine work, with less fanaticism. Edwin Muir – a great man, and writer – tried, but could not find any creative outlet in the use of Scots. Lewis Grassic Gibbon compromised, and used an English strongly salted with Scots words and speech-rhythms, with great success, in his "Scots Quair." He might have explored and developed this promising line of country but for his death at the age of 35: a tragic loss for Scottish literature.

But these are the very talented, the famous men. What of the ordinary scribblers, who have other work to do in daylight, and who must roam the Debateable Land by night – when it is more debateable that ever? Well, for myself, I like the Debateable Land! I've lived in it a good while now, and I doot I've ta'en ruit! But, as a last word on the subject: "Chucks-mei Scots!" and "Chucks-mei English" and "Chucks-mei a mixtur' of baith," when it happens to suit the theme, or rhymes better, or even just for the sheer perversity of it!

And the result . . .? Well, I'm sometimes reminded of a fine Scots poet of today, Sydney Goodsir Smith, saying "Chucks-mei!" about his sweetheart:-

> She talks an unco orra clash,
> But, och! It gleds ma ear;
> There's some may wale a wyce-like lass,
> Gie me ma daftie dear!"

Pleasures, places and people . . . . The choice could be endless, and finish up as a mere catalogue. And it was when I was looking about for some way of limiting my choice, and at the same time giving it a kind of frame to hold it together, that I came across a map I must have bought when I was a callant of fourteen or fifteen. It was my first large-scale map – Bartholomew's two miles to the inch series, Sheet Five, with a grand title, "Border Country." And there are enough pleasures, places and people associated with its roads and hills and waters, taken more or less at random to serve my purpose tonight – or a dozen nights. All the magical names were on my map – Eildon, Carterhaugh, Caerlanrig, Reidswire – and I'd nothing to do but grab a nibbie or loup on the bike and see them for myself. And wriggling down the brown contours, were burns I'd never even heard tell of, let along fished, till the day I first unfolded it. It was the map of the world as I knew it then, and it lived in pockets and fishing-baskets and bicycle-bags for years before it was retired, in favour of the lordly One-inch Ordnance series. But it keeps cropping up every now and again, as it did the other week.

> "Wad that I'd had as muckle care of getherin' gear
> As I've had, it seems, o' getherin' maps
> To guide ma stravaigin' feet owre Scotland!
> Maps . . .! Here they come at the spring-cleaning',
> Tummelin' oot o' the derk again . . . . Stour-getherers . . .
> Souchin' and flappin' like braithless concertinas . . . .
> Maps . . .! The kind o' thing weemen can never fauld richt,

Nae mair nor newspapers! Wi nae decorative value . . . .
Innerly, introspective sheets that hae nae look on bookshelves . . . .
That in thir days o' middle-age and scantit leisure,
Are gien an annual dicht, and daudit back again
Into the cupboard . . . .

And as I pit them back,
I can spare them a' a sigh . . . . toun and strath,
And ben and loch . . . . laich and howe and island . . . .
I micht gang there again, some day,
Ye can never tell . . . . And I pit them back.

But this Sheet, the sairest chowed o' them a',
I'll keep oot for a while . . Bartholomew . . "Border Country" . . .
It deserves better than the derk o' an aumry.
And gin I'd to wale but the yin, frae the haill slidderin' heap,
"Border Country" wad be ma choice . . . . ye can barely read the words on't,
"Border Country" . . . . dog-luggit . . . . tide-merked
Wi mony a drowe and drookin'; . . . .Forfochen at the seams
As a gangrel's troosers. A herbour for auld muillins
O' lang-forgotten pieces . . . . skurled wi' odd scales o' troot
Frae Merrylaw to Meggat, and wi' a nameless . . . bruckleness . . .
In yin corner (atween Lilliesleaf and Ancrum) that could be . . . .
That micht weel be . . . .that can hardly be ocht else than . . . .
The sair-dwined corpse o' a brammle worm!

Border Country!

And Tei'ot Stane pinpointed wi a dab o' jeely . . . .
The Thieves Road, and a route owre the hags o' The Roan
Scartit in wi' a pencil. And a merk, heich abune Hermitage,
For the Dinlay Spoot. An a merk on the shooder o' Cauldcleuch
To show where the cloudberries growe . . .. the daft berries
That ripen the wrang road roond in colour frae ocht else;
Frae reid to creamy-white . . . . Daft berries for daft days
O' wund and sun and rain, and the fer-away cryin' o' sheep,
The trinnle o' pule and stream . . . . the lost lease-haud o' youth
- But maimory's life-rent, to hain i' the hert for ever!

There's another thing I like about this old map of mine. It shows that there are two sides to the Border Country, for about a fifth of the map's area is in England. Flodden . . . .Cheviot . . . .Catcleuch Shin . . . . Peel Fell . . . . Bloody Bush . . . . Bewcastle . . . .! What map of the Border would be complete without Bewcastle, and Stanegirthside, where the Captain of Bewcastle lived? And a naisty sarcastic man he was, when he had Jamie Telfer o' the Fair Dodheid at his mercy:-

"Man, there's naething in thy hoose
But ae auld sword withoot a sheath
That hardly now wad fell a moose"

But if Jamie Telfer wasna juist a fair devil wi' the sword, my faith he could rin! In fact, he must have been the first Teviotdale Harrier! And the Captain got his paiks i' the end . . . .

A grand tale, "Jamie Telfer," with some real Border folk in it – like Auld Jock Grieve, for instance, keekin' oot o' the loft window at Colterscleuch wi' his pirnie on, and, even at that moment of stress and crisis, taking time to "redd-oot" his exact relationship to Jamie:-

"Alack a wae!" quo auld Jock Grieve,
"Alack! my hert is sair for thee!
"For I was married on the elder sister,
"And you on the youngest of a' the three."

Very characteristic of the Scots, this relationship business. But it can be carried to excess . . . . as in the Pittoddles family . . . .

"Well, ye see, auld Pittoddles, when his third wife dee'd, he got mairit on the Laird o' Blaithershins' aichteenth dochter, that was sister to Jemima that was mairrit till Tam Flemexer that was first and second cousin to the Pittoddleses, whase brother became Laird efterwards, and mairrit Blaithershin's Baubie – an' that way, Jemimabecam' in a kind o' way her ain niece and her ain auntie, an', as we used to say, her guid-brither was mairrit to his ain grannie."

But we're away up a close again. So let's get back to Scotland, Sheet Five:-

"Scotland Sheet Five is a square o' singin' waters
And names that are sangs, gin ye've a lug to hear:-
Coplaw Gair and Howdub, Crossbow and Braidleyhope,
Merrypath and Langtae, Byehass, Ladder Law,
Brunt Rig, Lamblair, Cauld Face, Blaeberry,
And . . . . Post Office Knowe . . . .

Whae named yon hill-top 'Post Office Knowe,'
Fer frae the haunts o' men,
Oot-bye Craik Cross abune Borthwick-heid?
- I'd fairly like to ken.

And whae brings the letters to Post Office Knowe,
Sae fer frae the haunts o' men?
A whaup wheels roond the pillar-box cairn,
Cryin, 'I dinna ken.'

Whae reads a' the cotton-gress postcairds there.

Sae fer frae the haunts o' men?
A black-faced yowe looks up frae her bite,
Beh-in' 'I dinna ken.'

They've a tod for telegraph-boy, nae doot,
Sae fer frae the haunts o' men,
And the grey hill-brock draws his pension there,
For ocht I ken.

The telephone linesman's a laverock there,
Fer frae the haunts o' men,
As he spiels up and doon his ledder o' sang,
Blithely, I ken.

But . . . . whae's postmaister on Post Office Knowe,
Sae fer frae the haunts o' men?
The wund gangs reeshlin' throwe the bents,
Cryin', 'I dinna ken . . . . I dinna ken . . . .
Unless it's . . . . Auld Nickie Ben'."

And so, ootbye beyond Post Office Knowe, and doon a burn I'll ca the Reuch Sike. A weel-kenned country fiddler leeved there, yince on a day. The Reuch Sike . . . . a guid name for a fiddler's howff, I've aye thocht, sin-syne. A name wi' a scrauch o' rosit in't, the skirl o' tormentit gut, and the bash and batter o' tackets on a country dancin' floor! Airchie o' the Reuch Sike . . . . Airchie the fiddler . . .

Airchie o' the Reuch Sike, ready for the set-tae,
Wi' blunt auld fingers calloused frae the howe,
Nid-nid-noddin', and the haill nicht afore him,
A hankie at his chowks, and a thick-broon chowe,
Nid-nid-noddin', and the merry fit tappin',
The merry fit tappin', that's quiet, now.

Airchie o' the Reuch Sike, scartin' Drops o' Brandy,
The whaups a' beddit, and ilk lamb and yowe
Snug aneth the staur-licht, the haill nicht afore him,
A gill inside his serk and a glint on his powe,
Nid-nid-noddin', and the merry fit tappin',
Airchie o' the Reuch Sike, gallus auld Airchie,
The lang nicht afore him, now.

And so across the hill and into Tima, and upper Dalgleish, where Adam Scott once lived, who was famous for the homely eloquence of his prayers at family worship. James Hogg has told us about them in "The Shepherd's Calendar," and let us remember that though they are quaint, they are none the less sincere:-

"For Thy mercy's sake – for the sake o' Thy poor sinfu' servants that are now addressing Thee in their ain shilly-shally way, hae mercy on Rob. Ye ken Yoursel he is a wild mischievous callant, and thinks nae mair o' committin' sin that a dog thinks o' lickin' a dish; but put Thy hook in his nose and Thy bridle in his gab, and gar him came back to Thee wi' a yerk that he'll no' forget the langest day he has to leeve.

Dinna forget puir Jamie, wha's fer away from among us, the nicht. Keep Thy airm o' power aboot him, and, oh, I wish Ye wad endow his wi' a like smeddum and spunk to act for himsel'. For if Ye dinna, he'll be but a bauchle in this world, and a backsitter in the neist.

We're a' like hawks, we're a' like snails, we're a' like slogie riddles; like hawks to do evil, like snails to dae guid, and like slogie riddles that let throwe a' the guid and keep the bad."

Who knows but that such prayers may have been the legacy of style from the famous Thomas Boston, who often visited Dalgleish when he was minister of Ettrick? And since we are so near, let us go down Tima to Ramsaycleuch, and up the road to "The heid o' Ettrick."

It was always a favourite place of mine; a dead-end road, and therefore spared the kind of visitor who leaves broken beer-bottles and Sunday papers strewn about the green shores of St. Mary's Loch, and makes puir Jamie Hogg, on his pedestal there, the goalkeeper for an impromptu soccer match!

Ettrick, with the hills crowding always higher and closer to the waterside, as you go up the glen . . . . Ettrick Pen, Wind Fell, Capel Fell . . . . all over 2,000 feet in height. "A wild region," Hogg called it, and the minister wrote in the First Statistical Account of 1792:-

"The roads are almost impassible. The only road that looks like a turnpike is to Selkirk . . . . In some places so deep as greatly to obstruct travelling. The distance is about sixteen miles and it requires four hours to ride it."

A wild region, sure enough, but it was bonny when I visited it one quiet Sunday afternoon last October. We stopped at Ettrick Kirk, and in the green kirkyaird they stand quite close together, the two graves, Boston's, the self-tormenting Calvinist, and James Hogg's, the herd-laddie of genius, and feckless farmer. Their deaths were separated by more than a century – Boston died in 1732 and Hogg in 1835 – but there was a strange link between these two vastly different men, for it was Hogg who took the very strong doctrine which Boston had preached, and revealed its potential dangers in a story that is a masterpiece of horror, "The Justified Sinner."

James Hogg has already been ably discussed by two speakers during the present session. "He was a great man," says Donald and Catharine Carswell, "who at his best could rival Burns in lyric poetry and excel Scott in prose." But a few words on Thomas

Boston may not come amiss, for he was a remarkable Borderer too.

Thomas Boston was born at Duns in 1676, and studied for three years at Edinburgh, where he fed his mind, and kept body and soul together for a total expenditure of £128 15s 8d Scots, or £11 18s 8d sterling. That sum included food and college dues – even 20 merks for his laureation. "By means thereof," he says, "I had a competent understanding of the logics, metaphysics, ethics and general physics." Not a bad educational bargain for less than £4 per year!

He was minister of Simprin Kirk – now a ruin – near Swinton in Berwickshire, from 1699 to 1707. When he preached at Whitsome, nearby, one Sunday, so large was his congregation that some of them clambered up to the thatched kirk roof, and tore away a portion of it in their eagerness to see and hear the preacher.

Mr Boston moved to Ettrick in 1707, where he was minister for a quarter of a century, till he died in 1732. He tells in his "Memoirs" how he fasted, how he exorcised ghosts, and how he wrestled in prayer. As he lost his teeth, he put them carefully away in a box, to be buried with him, so that he might rise complete at the resurrection. He describes his sins and his boils, his gravel, his scurvy, his colic, his journeys about his parish, his fears from Satan, and his perplexity when the dead-bell fell in the silence of the night, and came rolling and clanging downstairs. "The people of Ettrick," he says, "are great swearers but praying persons, notably smart and of uncommon assurance, self-conceited and censorious to a pitch."

When Mr Boston dispensed the Sacrament for the first time in Ettrick, there were present only 57 communicants. In 1731, when he dispensed it for the last time, there were 777. Crowds came as far as forty miles over the trackless boggy hills to hear him, and he was several times in trouble with his Session, over the problem of their board and lodging. "There are nine score strangers at Midghope," he says. "Four score of them, W. Blaik entertained . . . . and baked for them half a boll of meal for bread, bought 4/3d worth of bread, and killed 3 lambs and made 30 beds." A sair sanct for Ettrick hospitality Mr Boston must have been!

Now, one day about the year 1700, young Mr Boston espied a little book above the window-head of a house he was visiting in Simprin. It was called "The Marrow of Modern Divinity," printed in 1646, and brought home, he thought, by a soldier who had fought in the Civil War in England. "I relished it greatly," he says, "and . . . . purchased it from its owner. I regarded it as a light . . . . in my darkness." And having digested the strong doctrinal meat it contained, he began, from that time to preach it.

Seventeen years later, during discussion with some ministers of his own way of thinking, Mr Boston mentioned his little book. They were greatly delighted with it, and it was soon re-printed, with a preface by the minister of Carnock, "a man," says Boston, "of singular piety and tenderness." And strangely enough, his name was James Hog – spelt with one "g" only.

But the following year, the General Assembly found the little book's doctrine too extreme, and forbade it to be read.

The resultant "stour" in the Kirk gave rise to two new sets of the nicknames so dear to the heart of Auld Scotland – "anti-nomians" and "neo-nomians" – and the controversy, which was still raging years after Boston's death, took its name from his little book, being known as the "Marrow Controversy."

Now, I don't know anything about what used to be called "metapheesics." As a man once said – "Weel, Geordie, it's like this, ye see. When the yin that's listenin' doesna ken what the yin that's talkin' means; and when the yin that's talkin' doesna ken what he means himsel' . . . . that's metapheesics!" But the paragraphs in the Ettrick Shepherd's book describing the welcome of his "sinner" into the community of the "just, made perfect," are almost an exact paraphrase of a passage in Boston's little book. I won't quote them here but the resemblance is most striking. I don't know whether Hogg ever saw the book edited by his namesake, but he certainly understood the effects of its heady brew of doctrine on an ill-balanced mind:-

> "I wept for joy," he says, "to be thus assured of my freedom from all sin, and of the impossibility of my ever falling away from my new state. I felt as if I could have flown in the air, far above the earth. . . . . looking down with pity and contempt on the grovelling creatures below . . . "
> Then . . . . "I beheld a young man of a mysterious appearance coming towards me . . ."

The downfall of "The Justified Sinner" had begun.

And it is at least a possibility that if Mr Boston had not discovered his little book, Hogg's masterpiece would never have been written. It has been compared, to its advantage, with the work of Edgar Allan Poe and Daniel Defoe; and Andre Gide, the famous French writer, said that he had read it "with stupefaction and admiration that increased at every page . . . . I consider it an extraordinary achievement."

And there they lie at peace, the preacher and the poet, men of mark, in Ettrick kirkyaird. It would have been pleasant to have ended my visit with a longing to dwell there awhile, in the quiet of the green secluded glen. But there were some callants beyond the kirk dyke who found the silence oppressive. One lot were kicking a football about, with the usual hoarse cries of encouragement or derision. The other gang were having a "rock 'n' roll" session on an old sheet of corrugated iron; with every sign of enjoyment . . . . Aye, the world is never what it used to be, even in Ettrick of the high hills!

"Rock 'n' roll," I thought, as we went homeward down the narrow hill-road, "rock 'n' roll" – we may know what it means here and now, but it's going to need a footnote some day. Like "rock and reel" or "rockings," as they used to call the fun and frolic of barn and cottage which Burns knew, when the lasses brought their spinning with them. And the old bairns' game of "rockety-rowe," when two would stand back-to-back with their arms linked and by stooping alternately, raise each other from the ground chanting:-

"Wei butter, wei cheese,
Wei a pund o' cannle-grease,
Yowe up, mei doon,

That is the way to London toon."

And if I quoted Ecclesiastics:- "There is no new thing under the sun," it may have been because we were at that moment passing the Boston Memorial hall, where many a good "hoochin" country dance has sent the Ettrick hoolets mad with envy, and would have brought Thomas, whom it commemorates, striding down the road in a black fury of condemnation!

A wrathful preacher, but a kindly father, and a sick, puzzled man in his day, lang syne. And the heights were already rosy with the coming sunset, and the air clear and still, with the promise of frost, as we left Ettrick. It was the kind of night that James Hogg must have loved, for it was on such a night that he brought Kilmeny hame:

"When the freenge was reid on the wrestlin' hill,
The wud was sere, the mune i the wane,
The reek o' the cot hung owre the plain
Like a little wee cloud in the world its lane;
When the ingle lowed wi' an eiry leme,
Late, late in the gloaming Kilmeny cam hame."

I've always had a liking for stories about local characters; not those whose deformity of body or mind made them different, but the men of real originality, with a rough and salty wit, who enriched the life of neighbourhood with their foibles. And bless the men who took the time to write down the sayings and doings of these characters, and preserved them for the pleasure and instruction of later generations; men like Robert Murray in Hawick, and John Hyslop in Langholm and many another all over the country. For if the history books are the landscape art of the past, these local books are the intimate, "genre," painting of their period; the snapshots of an older time, with all the busy movement arrested, and the incident made memorable by its comedy. Scott knew and relished many of these characters, and used them in his novels, and he would have appreciated my favourite Hawick character, Wullie Gotterson, I'm sure. They were both volunteers, when Napoleon threatened invasion, and it was, in fact, on Wullie's field near Crumhaugh-hill that the local "False Alarm" beacon was lit.

Laird, "horse-couper" and farmer, Wullie was a familiar figure at all the horse-fairs of the Borders, clad in his grey top-coat, knee breeches, and "oot-steck" shoon. His property in Drumlanrig Square was known as "Gotterson's innery," a cluster of buildings with a kind of cesspool in the middle which he called "the silver lake." He was a popular landlord, but on one occasion he refused entry to a new tenant on the grounds that there were bugs in his furniture. After some argument, a Bailie was summoned, and the case laid before him informally. Having heard the story, the magistrate said, "And do you mean to say, Mr Gotterson, that you have no boags in your property?"

"Aw dinnae mean to say onything o' the kind," said Wullie. "Aw've owre mony already, and Aw dinna want ony mair!"

When his wife died, Wullie appeared for the funeral, clad in his blue wedding coat.

Some busybody wanted to know why he was not wearing the customary black garments, to which Wullie quietly replied, "Aw got her in blue, and Aw'll pairt wi'r in blue."

But my favourite of all the Gotterson stories is the one about his fight with a much bigger and younger man at the foot of the Loan. They had fallen out about the price of a horse, and the battle was fast and furious for a while, till Wullie was overborne, and went down in the gutter. His opponent was on top, but Wullie had a firm hold on his neck. One of the spectators said, "Ye hev the worst o'd, Wullie!"

"Oh," said Wullie, quite coolly, hanging on like a terrier, "Howt, man, it's lang or nicht!" At which remark, his enemy, thinking that the end of the struggle was a long way off, gave up, and went his ways. And if "What daur meddle wi' me?" illustrates their independence; "it's lang or nicht" isn't a bad motto for the sturdy tenacity of the Border breed.

I can't leave Hawick without mentioning Jock Weens, the cobbler, who had a small gift of prophecy. For when he was told that balloons would be the next form of travel, he said, "Aye, man, balloons? Balloons, think ee? My faith, but that'll habble the toll-bars!"

Robert Murray's book is a series of short sketches, but the other book I have in mind is a connected narrative, with the characters and stories woven into its fabric. John Hyslop wrote his reminiscences round about 1912. "Echoes from the Border Hills" gives a unique picture of life in a Border town, to which, because of its comparative isolation, change came slower than to most places. John Hyslop's style is as strong and comely as the buildings he erected at his family's trade of mason. His great-grandfather gave Thomas Telford, the famous civil engineer, his early training, at the building of Langholm Bridge, and the author, at the age of eighty-four, records stories he heard from his father and grandfather, so the book may be said to span the homely life of Langholm and Eskdale for nearly two centuries. The book is in our Public Library, but it is out of print and fairly expensive. I've heard of a Langholm man who had always wanted a copy, but did not succeed till he saw one for sale in Alexandria in Egypt during the war! . . . . Which reminds me of a leave spent in Naples, when I went into a book-shop on the Via Roma, and beheld there a complete set of Wilson's "Tales of the Borders." The Borders seemed a long way off, at that moment, and I thought of old John Hyslop's story of the Langholm man who went on a day-trip to Edinburgh soon after the railway opened. He spent the morning sightseeing, but by early afternoon he had become very homesick, and was wandering, disconsolate, on the slopes of the Calton Hill, when he came across a clump of nettles. This was too much for him, and he said to the familiar weeds, "Puir things, ee're like me'sel, fer frae hame!"

I have only time to select one character from the book, a local sage called Lancie Armstrong, who was as salty as they come. There was a relative of the Duke of Buccleuch mentioned in the newspaper, as being attached to the "commissariat department" of the army, and Lancie was asked by some weavers what this meant. He pondered a while, and said, "As fer as Aa can understand it, it's his job to po'or the tattas, and a' that sort o' thing."

Lancie caused much hilarity with his description of a public dinner he had attended, and his encounter with the first fully-dressed waiter he had ever seen, "a muckle falla," said Lancie, "wi' a dickie richt doon tae his breek-band heid." And when this dignitary offered Lancie red-currant jelly to go with his mutton, Lancie refused, saying, "Na, na, my man. I've never accustomed mesel to eat jam wi' butcher-meat."

Of spring-cleanings, which had come into fashion during his later years, Lancie said they were "an abomination of desolation" – a description which would be approved by a vast majority of men, then and now! And of the first cyclist he saw, he said, "Howt! It's never like the thing to sei a middle-aged man rinnin' aboot the country-side on a gird!"

The book is full of such characters; and with stories of fairs and hirings, wedding and funerals, kirks and markets, and mail-coaches, and a celebrity called Tam Robson, who "ran" with the post to Hawick. Tam set off with his letters and his fishing-rod, and fished his way up Ewes and "doon Tei'ot." And if the trout were on the take . . . . well, the letters were a wee bit late in getting to Hawick. But naebody seems to have been muckle the waur!

I can't leave Langholm without mentioning a man born there who has written some of our finest modern Scots poetry, C. M. Grieve, or "Hugh Macdiarmid." I remember discussing Macdiarmid's poetry once, with a well-known Scottish Nationalist who had been closely associated with him in the earlier days of the movement. We spoke of the poem, "Crowdieknowe," and I asked this Nationalist if he had ever visited Crowdieknow kirkyaird. He refused to believe that Macdiarmid hadn't invented the name; and when I showed it to him on the map, "owre the fer side o' Callister-ha'," he could hardly wait to go and see it for himself!

Langholm was full of nick-names in those days, and there was, in John Hyslop's time, a family called Laidlaw who had the queer by-name of "the gambies." Now, it may be hard to imagine a Langholm slave-trader – but there was one, and his name was Dr Laidlaw, sometimes written "Laidley." His trade, which was still quite respectable in the late eighteenth century, was carried on from his station on the river Gambia in West Africa, and when he died, his estate came to his relatives in Langholm, who were thereafter known as "the gambies."

Now, one day, a young man arrived at Dr Laidlaw's post on the Gambia. He came from the banks of another Border river, the Yarrow, and his name was Mungo Park. James Hogg, Scott, Leyden and Park were all born within the first six years of the seventeen-seventies. They were all remarkable men, but in some ways Mungo was the most remarkable of them all, in what he attempted and what he overcame, in his short life of thirty-five years.

Rumours of a "Great River" had haunted the fringes of Mediterranean history for over two thousand years. Centuries of travellers had gazed at the great barrier of the Sahara and wondered what lay beyond. We know now that the Niger rises less than 150 miles from the West African coast, flows towards the interior, then doubles back and completes a journey of 2,600 miles by entering the Atlantic through a vast delta into the Gulf of Guinea.

None of these facts was known to the tall muscular handsome young man in his early twenties who stepped aboard the brig "Endeavour" one day in 1795, nor to the English Africa Association who were sending him to replace their previous explorer who had been murdered. People who go exploring nowadays take truck-loads of equipment and provisions, medicines of all kinds, cine-cameras, and radio-sets. Mungo Park set out to discover the Great Mysterious River, dressed in a blue coat with brass buttons, and a beaver tile hat. He had letters of introduction to Dr Laidlaw, a letter of credit for £200, an umbrella, a pocket sextant, a thermometer – not a clinical one – and a few changes of linen.

Mungo arrived on the Gambia, and stayed with Dr Laidlaw for several months, during which he studied the local language and had his first bout of fever. Then, at the beginning of December, he set off on horseback with two slaves and a few fellow-travellers, clad in the blue coat, tile hat and nankeen trousers. He had provisions for two days, some beads and tobacco to buy more food, two compasses, the other articles I have mentioned, and two fowling-pieces and a pair of pistols. Waving farewell to Laidlaw, who never expected to see him again, he rode off into the jungle on what might fairly be called "Operation Tile Hat," or "Exploration Strip-tease." And the strip-tease began quite soon, for some village women tore the brass buttons from his coat.

On his arrival at Bondou, he presented the local king with some trade goods and his umbrella. "I put on my new blue coat in order to preserve it," says Mungo. But this canny plan went agley, for the king, Almani, although quite pleased with the umbrella, took a great fancy to the new coat. Nothing else would please him. Mungo thought about the Mysterious River, slowly took off the coat, and laid it at the king's feet. He was allowed to pass on.

By Christmas Eve, Mungo had arrived at Joag. But he had passed through a kingdom without paying customs-dues or making a present to the king. Some horsemen from the monarch arrived at the explorer's hut, seized his baggage, tore it open, and departed with half of his possessions. The situation was serious. Mungo had nothing left to trade for food on the long journey that lay ahead, except a few beads and some amber. His slaves begged him to turn back, and he sat all day, hungry, considering what to do. An old slave-woman, passing by, took pity on him, and gave him a handful of ground-nuts. Then a guide turned up, the son of a neighbouring king. Mungo put on his second-best blue coat, and set off again, reached the Senegal river, and got safely across. His princely guide now required a present. Mungo gave him 14/- worth of amber and tobacco.

And so he arrived in the kingdom of the pleasantly-named ruler, Tiggity Sego, who didn't rob him directly, but sent his son, Mungo's guide, to borrow his horse. Mungo had to hang about, well into January, before he got it back. As he prepared for departure, he was invited to contribute another present. He again offered amber and tobacco, but this wasn't enough for the king's son. He and his party flung themselves on Mungo's baggage, gathered up about half the contents, and went off, laughing.

Three-quarters of the explorer's luggage had now disappeared; there were rumours of war in the district; but it was already two months since he had left the coast, and the Niger was still far distant. He continued his journey, and arrived, presently, in the kingdom of Kaarta. Here, he had to leave his only blanket as payment for food and lodging.

The blue coat and the black tile caused quite a sensation in the kingdom of Kemmoo, but the king, a decent chap by the name of Daisy Koorabarra, advised Mungo to turn back. He did not want a white man murdered in his country. Mungo thanked him politely for his advice – and asked for a guide. He got one; and sent the Daisy his horse-pistols, having, he says, found weapons of little use in his travels!

In the next village, robbers stole some of his clothes, beads and amber. Mungo accepted the situation, and rode on, arriving next on the borders of the kingdom of Ludamar, where his predecessor, Major Houghton, had been murdered. Here, he paused, to send a present of five cotton garments to the Emir Ali, and waited a fortnight for permission to pass through his kingdom. When no reply came, he decided to go on, and on March 1st, he reached Deena, where he was very roughly handled by the Moors who spat upon him, and took what they fancied from his luggage. He left the place in haste, at two in the morning, his only companion now being his black slave, Demba. At Dallie, the next village, he dallied a while, and was being regaled with some excellent beer, when a band of Moors arrived on horseback. Ali the king had decided to show the white man to his wife Fatima. Mungo had no choice. He gathered up his scanty gear and went with them.

The capital, Benown, was a town of tents. Mungo got a sullen reception from Ali, and the subtle present of a young wild pig. The idea was that pigs must hate Christians as devourers of their flesh, so the pig was released in the hope that it would bite Mungo. This pig, however proved to be pro-Christian, and ran amok, biting every Moor it encountered. The joke was over.

For days afterwards, Mungo was tormented, reviled, spat upon. Never once did he allow himself to lose his temper. He wanted to reach the Niger. He buried one of his compasses in the sandy floor of his tent. Without a compass he was utterly doomed. Next morning he was searched and stripped of all his gold, amber, his watch and second compass. Of these, only the compass was returned. He was now alone, without a change of clothes, baggage or horse, but with two compasses.

For months, Mungo remained a prisoner, through sandstorms, unbearable heat, fever and constant hunger. But at last the court journeyed north to the queen. She took quite an interest in Mungo, and gave him a bowl of milk. And this kindly woman was at last instrumental in getting him back part of his belongings. He had tried to escape, and had been re-captured. When he got some of his clothes back, he tried again, and this time he was successful. Mungo's wardrobe now consisted of two shirts, two handkerchiefs, two pairs of trousers, an inner and an outer waistcoat, a pair of half-boots, and his tile hat. He had no money, and nothing to trade with, but he still went on. When he was refused food by a chief, he had learned to go to the poorest quarter of the village, and never was he turned away empty.

His horse was now in low condition, and he had to cut some brass buttons from his waistcoat for a small bag of corn to feed it. He had better luck with his next few villages, but he had little left worth stealing. Dodging lions and wolves, he journeyed steadfastly on. And now comes a story-book touch. At a small village, he traded one of his last brass buttons for some food. Next day, he came to a wide stretch of marshland. And beyond the marsh-land . . . . there was a river.

"I saw the long sought-for majestic Niger, *flowing to the east,* and glittering to the morning sun, as broad as the Thames at Westminster ..." Almost a pre-echo of a famous sonnet, there, but Mungo had neither Wordsworth's skill in letters nor, by now, his cosy view of natural history.

He went on to explore part of the great river, but at last he had to turn aside and try to make his way back to the coast. The rainy season had begun. But before he had gone very far, robbers waylaid him in the jungle, cut off his last brass button, then stole his tile hat and all his remaining clothes. He had reached the Niger, and now Africa seemed to be demanding the end of the strip-tease in payment. After some parley, he managed to get back the more ragged of his two shirts and trousers, but the thieves drove away his horse. Desperately he shouted after them – for his tile hat! The robber paused, and weighed the hat in his hand. It was heavy and uncouth. He flung it back and disappeared into the forest.

A few moments later, this amazing Borderer stood alone in the wilds of Africa. He was five hundred miles from the nearest European settlement, without a horse, weapons or money, and clad in a ragged shirt and breeks – completely abandoned, with the jungle rain pouring down on his bare head. Africa seemed to have won. But he picked up his tile hat and put it on. It was more than a symbol of the civilisation he still hoped to see again; all his notes and travel records were hidden away in the crown! He continued his journey.

It was a June night before he saw again the other river of his dreams, the Yarrow, and knew that he had won the round after all; the first round. The second round, that was to be Africa's, was years ahead yet, as he made his way up to Foulshiels from Selkirk. The braes of Yarrow would be bonny, in the endless June twilight; much more to his taste than the stifling streets of London, where he had been praised, but where he had proved to be too restrained and shy to become a popular hero.

And maybe his welcome home to Yarrow was enough to please him. It was, in many ways, a welcome typical of Scotland and the Scots. For when Mungo reached the little whinstone house at last, and knocked, his mother heard the sound and wakened his brother who farmed the place, saying, "Get up, Airchie! There's a man chappin' at the door!"

"Oh, aye," yawned Airchie, turning over in bed, tired after a busy market-day. "I daursay that'll be oor Mungo. I saw him getting' off the coach in Selkirk, the day."

So Mungo came home. And the tile hat . . . . ? it would be pleasant to think that it had been preserved for posterity. But there seems to be no record of its fate. Like another lum-hat, it probably floated away down to the sea, "wantin' the croon," for Mungo was not a sentimental man. He was to show, in fact, during his second expedition to Africa that he could be ruthless. But I think he was, in his way, a great man; a man whose motto might well have been those words of Wullie Gotterson's, "It's lang or nicht."

Places . . . . People . . . . Pleasures . . . . The pleasures that are creative, even in a small way. The Scots have a word for them: "ploys." And since the ploy I've chosen has a Scots name too, maybe this is how an old hand at the game might tell you about it:-

When the back-end wunds have stripped the wuds bare, and the last ragments o' leaves are birlin' slowly doon: that's the time to gaun for nibbie-sticks!

Now, a nibbie-stick's no' juist another name for a walkin'-stick. A walkin'-stick's either an article o' commerce or a work o' art. The commercial kind are pairt o' the stock-in-tred o' maist bacca-shops, and as like-other as peis in a swad. The artistic kind can be seen at agricultural shows and sic-like, wi' horn hannles kerved into a' kinds o' whurly-whas, and glitterin' wi' verneesh. They're magnificent, but they're no' nibbies! A nibbie's no' juist for helpin' ye owre the grund. It's for slashin' at nettles, rattlin' alang railin's – or even fellin' a pheasant if ye're that way inclined!

Compared wi' a nibbie, a walkin'-stick's nae better than a palin'-stob: for a *richt* Nibbie has aye a kinnin' o' the yauldness o' life left in't. And there's mony a less pleasant and mair fashious way o' spendin' a caller wunter efternune, than bi slippin' a little saw and a trowel into eer pooch and off to the wuds, and, sune, ye're daunderin' alang gledgin' aboot frae yin side to the t'other as ye gaun. There's nae hurry. That's yin o' the chiefest pleasures o' nibbie-huntin'; for a nibbie's never been kent to rin away!

But a word o' wairnin' here! Make gey shuir ye have the place till eersel: for onybody, comin' by, micht think eer antics were a bit by-ordinar! Aa mind yince o' sei-in a wice-like esh-plant that was growin' on a steep cley bankin', an' Aa wasna owre keen to gaun doon, till Aa kent it was guid enough. So Aa stude and lookit at it for a bit, and Aa keekit at it – first frae the yin side, and then the t'other – to make shair it was strecht. Then, juist when Aa'd hunkert doon to sei in-ablow a brainch, Aa heard geeglin'! And when Aa lookit roond, Aa saw twae lassies comin' alang the path, fair soople! So Aa went off in a hurry, gey affrontit! But Aa cam' back later on, mind ye, and got the nibbie!

And so, sometime on eer walk, ye come on a beauty. The stem's as strecht as a resh, wi verra few twigs on't. It's juist aboot the richt thickness; neither owre wauf nor owre solid, and the bairk's a smooth cule grey, withoot a merk or a flaw. So ye oot wi eer trowel and stert clearin' the soil away, till ye can sei if the ruit hes the richt bend; and on a bankin', there's mair chance that it wull, than on level grund.

And this is a guid yin ye've gotten, wi an interestin' birl, where the ruit's hed to wun roond a stane. So, yince the soil's cleared, cut the side-ruits wi' the saw, gangin' gey canny, for the bairk's soft ablow grund. Then ease the plant oot, and it's yours, and ye've naething mair a-dae but sned off the twigs, and away home, throwe the gloamin' o' the bare-brainched wunter wud, wi eer nibbie.

A wesh at the kitchen sink clears the cley off't, and a pickle off er-sel as weel Then lay't aside for a while to let the bairk set. Efter that, ye can feenish't off at the fireside, bendin' oot the bits o' kinks, and shapin' the hannle to eer fancy. Then a rub wi' sandpaper – and a ferrule, mebbe, if ye're the kind that likes to gaun clankin alang a road. But nae verneesh!... No' for mei, onyway! And there's eer nibbie!

There's only yin difficulty left now. How to get rid o'd . . . . for yince it gets haud o' ye as a ploy, ye can never sei a wud for the nibbies that's in't, and it's nae time afore ye've fer owre mony! Ye sei, it's a hard job to walk wi' mair than yin at a time And even withoot ferrules, they take a while to wear oot! In fact, wi' aboot hauf a dizzen, ye're set up for life!

But they're no' sae easy to gie away as ye micht think. Folk'll say, "Oh, Aa hev a nice walkin'-stick already, wi' a silver mount, thenk ye." And it's nae guid tryin' to tell them that it's a *nibbie* ye're offerin' them, no' juist a walkin'-stick. Aa've fund that yin o the best ways is to leave them ahint when ye veesit folk – and even then, ye whiles get them handit back, the next time ye ca' . . . . It's a problem, Aa tell ye! And, it's a kinda shame to use them for pei-sticks, after a' eer work.

Howanever . . . . another back-end comes roond, the leaves come birlin' doon, and afore ye ken where ye ir, ye're off – aye, even though somebody at Copshaw Holm , that heard ye were interested, has juist sent ye hauf o' his late grandfaither's collection o' twae hunder nibbies . . . . ye're off to the wuds again, and the cry is "Excelsior"! Or, to be perjink, "Fraxinus Excelsior." And, efter a;, that's juist the botanical name for an esh-plant – the raw material for another nibbie-stick!

And so – and maybe no' afore time! – we take a last look at the tattered map, and note, before we fold it away, that Mr Bartholomew made a good job into a masterpiece by placing, bang in the middle of it, the town in which we are known to take so modest a pride! And what better-loved landmark have we than: "The Vertish":-

Ye may ken, I was born and bred i' the Loan,
In a yin-end whunstane biggin',
Wi' an ootlook on to the Bleachin' Green
And Back-brae craws on the riggin';
A guid-gaun lum for a wunter's nicht,
Wi' my feet on the polished fender –
But they cam' and condemned it, and garred mei flit –
Mei! A born Wast-ender!

I work away i' the spinnin'-mill
Up to the cuits in ooder.
But I'm fain for a sicht o' the Vertish Hill
Wi' his plaid flung owre his shooder.
His waistcoat and breeks o' comely green,
The wud hei weers like a croon.
And I mind o' the days that yince hae been
And ma hert's sair cuissen-doon.

For now o' The Loan that I used to ken
There's hardly a stannin' stane;
Even my douce auld neebor The Moat
Looks muckle to mean and lane –
But *hei* has the Vertish to bield his back,
And keep things a' in order . . .
There's higher hills? Aye! But where'll ye sei
A bonnier view o' the Border?

Man . . . Ocht worth tippence gaun on i' the toon
Aye comes there, sune or later –
Cornets and Callants and mairchin' bairns –
It's a local law o' natur'!
Golfers and sledgers and dydie-eggs,
Or auld folk seekin' a sate
O' a simmer's nicht; the Hill's aye there
And his welcome never blate.

So . . . just dinna let-on if ye sei mei nod
Guid-nicht, to my freend owre thonder,
As dowie I gang for the Burnfit bus,
For mony's the time I ponder;
How is't that yon humphie-backit hicht
Can steer up thochts sae tender?
For there's never a hill like the Vertish Hill
To a guitter-bluid Wast-ender!

There have been many who have sung of Border people, places, and pleasures, but none, I'm sure, more tunefully than William Landles, whose work is receiving growing recognition, these days. Here is a sample from the second book of verse he has published:-

LAIRD AND HAUFLIN

Wi' a seep, seep, and a dreep, dreep,
This mony an 'oor,
The rain's steadily faa'n, faa'n
In an eendoon poor.
Says the auld laird – "We'll hae nae crap,
This drookit year."
Thinks the hauflin up in the bothy –
"But it's snug here!"

The sun's scowderin' sair, sair
On the laigh raws:
And brunt broon in the lang droot
Are the neep shaws.
Says the auld laird – "We'll be hard fashed
For the want o' weet."
But the hauflin streeks on the knowe back
In the day's heat.

The frost's gruppen the ferm groun'
Wi' a ticht haun'
And the auld laird stappin' hamewan',
Is a soored man.
But oot yont 'neth the mune's licht,
At the coortin' thrang,
The hauflin kens that the warld's sweet
And there's noucht wrang.

And another local writer, David Johnston, whose skilful verses on all manner of themes delight us so often. Mr Johnston is an expert with the "Habbie" stanza that Burns was so fond of using, but my choice tonight is in a simpler scheme:-

JENNIE

She cam' tae my door when the frost and the snaw
Had nae ither thocht but tae nither us a';
Tae the warmth o' my boiler I beckoned her in.
And that was hoo twa he'rts were rowed intae yin.

And noo ilka day she ca's in while I wark,
Tho' black is my face like my breeks and my sark,
And no' a bit backward she sits on my knee,
As muckle in common hae Jennie and me.

Sae fair is her form and sae bricht are her een,
They shine like the dewdraps that glint on the green;
Attired in a cloak o' a licht reddish-broon,
I vow she's the handsomest lass in the toon,

And, loons, here's a secret I'm gaun tae loot dab,
If time ye will gie me to open my gab;
Ne'er judge you a lass by the shape o' her mou',
Her tongue micht no' answer the cut o' your shoe.

But that isna Jennie, and that isna Grace,
And, Lord, I am thankfu' there's nocht oot o' place,
For while I hae Grace tae assist me life thro',
I'll aye hae a crust for my little broon doo.

And, to conclude, a poem by a grand old lady who wrote in the fine Scots tradition of Grisel Baillie, Alison Rutherford, and Jean Elliot: a lady who mended the words and wrote the music of one of our best-loved songs, "Annie Laurie." Lady John Scott was born five years before Waterloo, yet she lived into the first spring of the present century. And here is her welcome to a season we are all looking forward to:-

MOORLAND SPRING

There's no a muir in my ain land but's fu' o' sang the day,
Wi' the whaup, and the gowden plover, and the lintie upon the brae.
The birk in the glen is springin', the rowan-tree in the shaw,
And every burn is rinnin' wild wi' the meltin' o' the snaw.

The wee white cluds in the blue lift are hurryin' light and free,
Their shadow fleein' on the hills, where I too fain wad be;
The wind frae the west is blawin', and wi' it seems to bear
The scent o' the thyme and gowan thro' a' the caller air.

The herd doon the hillside's linkin'. O, licht his heart may be
Whose step is on the heather, his glance owre muir and lea!
On the moss are the wild ducks gatherin', whar the pules like diamonds lie,
And far up soar the wild geese, wi' weird, unyirdly cry.

In mony a neuk the primrose lies hid frae stranger een,
An' the broom on the knowes is wavin' wi' its cludin o' gowd and green.
Owre the first green sprigs o' heather, the muir-fowl faulds his wing,
And there's nought but joy in my ain land at the comin' o' the spring.

OBSERVATIONS

OBSERVATIONS
HAB o' HAWICK

Birdsong

Hab wasna a bit pleased to see the Post Office engineers plantin a raw of muckle black telephone poles alang the backs o the gairdens. He was stan'in at his back door, ca'in them blots on the landscape, an waur names as weel, when a mavis cam and lichtit on the top o yin pole and syne a blackie on the top o another. And afore lang, the per o them were tirlin away as if they'd been trained a' their days to dae nocht less but trespass on Post Office property, bless their herts.

It was a soft nicht, and birdsang seems to traivel better wi a souch o rain i the air. Hab was fell pleased wi the soond, but the way the rain wad gar the weeds come daudin up in his gairden chastened his elation.

Whatever gars birds sing, I dinna ken, says Hab. They used to say that it was because they were pleased wi life, but there's a new theory gaun aboot that makes oot that each yin sings a kind o personal national anthem to let a' the other birds ken to keep on the fer side o the frontier. A welsh kind o theory that. Hab still thinks they sing because they enjoy singin. They thraw nae temperament, their percentage o the takins is twae-threi wire-worms or sic-like things that we can weel spare, and they-re at hame on ony platform.

Nae doot, says Hab, lookin at the telephone poles, nae doot mavis and blackie sang on the top o the Jeddart gibbets i' the auld days, when a wheen gallant mosstroopers had been yerkit and the corps hingin in cheens, mebbe!

A macHABre thocht, says I, but Hab juist grumphed something aboot a verra laboured pun and went away in.

Cricket

Hab never paid to see a cricket match in his life, but his wife says he's turned a perfect scunner since the Test matches stertit. Sits wi his lug (the guid yin) again the speaker whenever there's a commentary on, though fine he kens that his tattas need settin up.

Wheesht, wumman – that's aboot a' she can get oot o'm, but when he daubit his bonnet at her when she askit what kind o beast a silly mid-on was, she realised that he was gey fer gane, and that she'll juist hev to thole, and hope it wadna be smittal.

Hab says it's a game played against the wather, the same as gairdenin, and there's aboot the same element o uncertainty in baith, namely 99.9 per cent. Then, even if the wather's a'richt, there's blichts, scabs, pests, and cusha-dowes to content wi.

And what's the cricketin equivalent of thaim? I speired.

As far as the Australians are concerned, Bedser! But dinna keep me bletherin here, says Hab. Arlott'll be on ony meenit now.

Nipknowes Idyll

Hab was fell taen on wi the big photograph on the front page o a recent "The Weekly Scotsman." It showed the Cornet, the big gallop owre and the Flat safe and soond. His tile hat's away owre the back somewhere and he's lookin at the staff o the Flag as if he was thinkin that here was a meenit o his life he wad like to lest for ever.

It's a place there's a photo taken thrae every 'eer, says Hab, but it's the only yin I've seen that fair pits the whole speerit o the Common Riding in a nutshell. The camera's mebbe a machine, but in the hands o a skilled operator it can tell a story and stop Auld Time himself, deid in his tracks. So there's the Coronation Common Riding captured forever wi a flick o the shutter. The sun's beginning to shine, the Richt and Left are close ahint, and the lave o the followers are weel strung oot doon the links o the road There's a fine fluther o hedge-parsley creamin owre the fence like a wave o the sea, and a glimpse o yon auld battered dyke that rins at intervals up the hill. A guid place for wild strawberries yon, when I was a callant. They're in blossom there, and buttercups and cranesbill and vetch on the gressy verge o the white simmer road, and breckans the derk o the wud.

Further doon, says Hab, getting his braith back, there's a fine glitter o cars on the Vertish, and away below, there's the ancient toon o Hawick, steeple and lum an a' doverin, already in a kind o sunny dwam, and in process o temporary evacuation There's even a lazy puff o steam thrae an engine doon aboot the station somewhere that indicates to the discernin ei that the trains are in the strunts and dinna care whether they rin or no'.

But ye canna see a' that list o floo'ers on the photograph, says I.

Mebbe no, says Hab. But they're there, nane the less, and twae-threi mair I dinna ken the names o'.

How d'ye ken? says I.

Because I went up special, to look, says Hab. But there's yin thing there that wasnae there on Chase morning.

And what's that?

A bookie's ticket, torn in twae, says Hab. It's a' by for another 'eer. But we've aye the photo to mind us on.

Alibi

Hab saw something in the paper the tother day aboot ice-cream flavoured wi port sherry, whusky and sic-like alcoholic beverages. Some ministers in Glesca thocht it was a "subtle peril." Hab can hardly wait.

No' that I'm a lover o ice-cream, says Hab. But juist think o the expression on the wife's face when I came doon thrae the Muir in kinda guid fettle and say, No, now, I've never been <u>near</u> the Feraway Tent. I've juist been mixin my sliders!

Clocks

The tother morning, efter a herty supper o young ingins and lettuce, Hab slept-in hal an oor, and was gey sair putten-tilt to get to his work in time, so he was in a bad tuin a' forenuin.

When he had recovered efter dinnertime, and was yince mair fit to be spoken till, somebody suggested he should get an alairm clock.

Nane o yon things for me, says Hab. I dinna like modern clocks at a'. They're symptomatic o the times we leeve in. Thaim alairms clatter and batter a hunder to the dizzen, till yin canna get slept. They're that efficient, it fair scunners a body. Gie me a guid-gaun grandfaither clock. Yon lang case is built wi the same idea as the soond-box o a fiddle – to gie sonority to the music o the movement as weel as to accommodate the lang, leisurely pendulum.

Yon auld clock o mine, says heigh, howe, heigh, howe, as if it was commiseratin wi mankind for the passage of time. It's a dignified, resonant, drowsy tick, that reminds yin o the importance o sleep as a repairer o human stresses and strains. And there's gey often a nice bit decoration roond aboot the dial as weel. Mine has some gold whurlie-whas, and a verra nate little picture o Tam o Shanter and Souter Johnnie busy at the yill-stakes - mebbe a subtle reminder that nae man can tether time. Aye, and grandfaither clocks were made, or putten the-gither, at wice-like places like Langholm, or Jethart – no' in Amairica or Switzerland and orra places like that.

And mind this, says Hab, knockin oot his dottle, mind this: My grandfaither clock ticks twae to an alairm-clock's dizzen, but for a' the clatter and batter, the hands juist take the same time to gang roond the oor. There's a moral there for somebody, but I henna time to tell ye what it is, the now.

"Mirriest of Nichtis"

This is a time o 'eer that I like weel, says Hab, when it's never richt derk at nicht. It aye pits me in mind o the openin lines o William Dunbar's poem, "The Twa Mariit Wemen and the Wedo," where he sets the scene

> "Upon the Midsummer evin, merriest of nichtis,
> ....neir as midnicht was past,"

In that kind o enchanted green licht o midsummer in Scotland that comes for sic a short time to repay us for a' the derk and weet, the glaur and rouk, o wunter.

The time for enchantments in Scotland has lang been fixed at Hallowe'en, but they're din, boogly enchantments, wi a guff o wat strae and neeps and a glisk o brumstane, at that dreich time o eer. The magic o midsummer is a green mystery, airy and fresh wi growin gress and hedges lood wi linties. And there the twae wives and the wedo sit, wi their "cleir hair" kaimed owre their young shooders, garlanded in floo'ers, cled in bonny green mantles, forever owre-heard at their scandalous crack by Auld Dunbar ahint the hedge, i the oors when the licht never fades beyond the under-water twilicht o a clear-rinnin burn.

But maist o us, says Hab, snore away nichts like this in juist the same way as we dae in dowie November. But we're sweir into bed; we're inclined for last looks at the gairden. Mebbe we ken that the "mirriest" of nichtis has been lost.

Speed

Hab was away up bye Newmill the tother day when it cam on a gey heavy thunner-plump. He was juist lookin roond for a place to shelter when a muckle lang car stoppit and a man wi horn-rimmed glesses stuck his heid oot. "You wanna ride into town?" he said. Hab graciously assented, and as he was getting into the back seat, an auld tramp cam shauchlin bye. The American hesitated for a meenit, then he hailed the tramp as weel. "You wanna ride?"

The tramp stoppit and conseedert the offer. The rain was comin doon hard and his threadbare shooders were already beginning to darken wi weet. The American began to fidget. "C'mon" he said, already half-regrettin the offer, "I gotta hurry."

"No," said the tramp, gledgin up in a bleery kind o way. "No thanks."

Whaffor?" asked the astonished visitor, mebbe a kenning relieved, for it was a gey dirty-like gangerel.

"Weel," says the tramp, "I'd juist get to some place afore there was ony need for't."

Hab watched the folorn feegur dwindling on the rain-lashed road as the huge car gathered speed.

"See that one of your planes clipped some more time off the Paris trip." chatted the American as they roared along. "Paris in twenny minutes. Now that's progress, ain't it?"

Sure is, says Hab.

Mushrooms

There's nae tellin, wi mushrooms, says Hab. Some folk say that they growe best in dry simmers. Others say that a wat eer's the best. For mysel', I think that a wat airly simmer and a dry August are the best condeetions, but I'm nae authority. In fact I'm no a great lover o mushrooms at a'. But I canna resist lookin for them. Even efter I've hed a fry or twae and stew, I dinna care if I never see another on my plate for a twalmonth, but I still gang lookin for them. Shairly mush-huntin is yin o the maist hermless sports gaun. In how fer a mushroom suffers throwe bein pulled and flung into a pan, I couldnae say, but I wadna say it added muckle to the sum-total o the world's pain.

It's a fine healthy sport, is mush-getherin. It gets yin airly oot o bed and raikin owre auld pastures wi the dew fresh on the gress, and say what ye like, it's the best o the day. Folk whiles laugh at me because I aye take a per o binoculars when I gang for mush, but it has saved me mony a weary fit lookin at yon flat heids o' the flo'oers ca'd yarrow, hanks o wool, and even white stanes. But when a fermer pits doon a load o lime-stane in a field, then I gie up a' thegither, it's waur than a needle in a haystack.

Railway Stations

Big stations are a' verra weel in their way, says Hab. There's naething I like better than a look roond Waverley, especially when the Flyin Scotsman's getting ready to leave, and a' sorts and condeetions o traivellers are bustling aboot wi bags and trappins. And there was aye a thrill when the nicht Pullman cam birlin roond the bend, and ye were off throwe the derk hills, wi a last gledge at St Mary's clock keekin owre the ruifs like a sma local mune.

But my favourite stations are the yins where even a stopping train halts for only a contemptuous meenit, where the station-maister has verra obviously juist laid doon his howe and put on his offeecial coat and hat when he heard the signal wires gurrin. And afore the train's weel roond the next curve, he's back at his neeps, leavin't to the tow-heidit laddie that takes eer ticket to note for reference which airt ye turn when ye gang oot throwe the yett.

They've a' got personalities of their ain, have stations, but I only ken twae that have onything unco aboot them. Yin o them's Reston Junction, a place I havene seen for eers, but I suppose it's a normal enough station to the outward eye. Yet there was a Hawick wumman used to take a flyin-oot lip whenever the train got to Reston Junction, every August Holiday withoot fail. At Chirnside she was juist like a'body else i the cairrage, but afore the train got stoppit at Reston, there she wad be pootin', like an auld bull troot, wi' a' her freends trying to make up their minds whether it was a juidgment or juist the strong sei air seepin up thrae aboot Eyemooth.

The tother by-ordinar station I have in mind is Riccarton. Now Riccarton, to some folk, is juist a godless plot o railway-lines, a limbo for locomotives, clappit doon withoot regaird for the comfort o man nor beast on the top o a bare hill. But there was aye something queer and uneasy aboot it that I could never understand till yin day I was owre at the Nine-stane Rig. It was then I fund oot that the Stanes keep an eye on the Station, and the Station keeps an eye on the Stanes, and the Stanes, though gey decrepit and sair neglectit, have a decided edge on the Station, on account o hevin been there a sicht langer. And, furthermair, they intend to be there a guid while efter the Station's been taen up by the ruits and thrawn away.

This century-auld cat and moose ploy has had a bad psychological effect on the Station, and sensitive guairds on goods-trains say that the balefu influence o the Stanes can be felt as fer doon as Deidwaitter. But it's mair obvious, of course, on the main line. Ye'll have noticed how aggressively the trains huff and puff a' the road up to Riccarton thrae Copshaw Holm? A defence mechanism, as shair as daith, says Hab.

Aye, the engines whussle defiantly, and try to hide the Station ahint their black reek, but they maun gang their gaits. The smoke-screen blaws away. And yince mair there's silence. And owre on the Rig, the grey, basilisk stare o the waitin stanes.

Observation: Expect nothing, and when good occurs to you
Look on it as "A Sign of Grace."

Observation. Sunday 7th November

Glooms and glints, sudden flashes of gold across the fields – teuch and smooth on grass, brittle and fragmented over stubble. Hazy vistas, lit gables and glowing stone, texture of harled walls accented by shadows cast by pebbles from oblique sunlight. Sombre hedges crimson lit by haw-heavy twigs and boughs. The way sunlight picks out objects at this time of year – a tree in thinning leafage, spotlit, while all the rest of the field or bank lies deep in shadow.

NIBBIE-STICKS

SIMPLE PLEASURES
"NIBBIE – STICKS"
by David Hill

15 - minute Talk.

A week or two ago, the woods were aflame with scarlet, orange, and gold, but the fires of autumn have faded now. Slowly and sadly, the last leaves spiral down in the still blue air of a frosty afternoon. And once more the time comes round to arise and go in search of nibbie-sticks.

A nibbie-stick, in my part of Scotland, isn't the same thing as a walking-stick. A walking-stick is art; a nibbie-stick is as nearly natural as possible. I yield to no one in my admiration for the walking-sticks one sees at agricultural shows, gleaming with varnish, with glassy-smooth horn handles garnished with thistles, their stems carved and coloured – they are magnificent, but they are not nibbies. A nibbie is meant for helping you over the ground, for slashing at nettles, for rattling along railings – a fiendish compulsion! – and, in extreme cases for knocking a rabbit cold. Certain nefarious nibbies have been known to have salmon-cleeks attached to them, but, as they say in the cinema, "I wouldn't know about that".

Nibbie-sticks are of different woods and varying weights according to the mood you're in, the kind of country you're walking, and the season of the year. And there are many less pleasant and more complicated ways of occupying a crisp November or December afternoon than by slipping a small saw and a trowel into the pocket of an old suit and making for the woods.

The best breeding-grounds for nibbies are the sloping banks of a river or burn-side. Beneath you, the water chuckles quietly in a wintry dream, tree and sapling have a bare and lightsome beauty of line after the dense foliage of summer has been shed, and you can amble peacefully along over a rustling carpet of leaves, stalking, so to speak, your stick. Soon, you spy a likely-looking ash-plant further down the bank, and make for it, but on closer inspection it turns out to have a badly-kinked stem, or the bark has been scarred – no good. But you can afford to be both philosophical and fikey; it is a long wood, and you have an hour or two in hand. So you prowl onward, looking this way and that.

Solitude, I may say, is essential. The uninitiated spectator is apt to find nibbie-stacking comical. I once stopped to look at a promising nibbie a few yards down a steep bank which I did not want to descend until I was sure that my quarry was up to standard. So I viewed it carefully from where I stood, harked forrard, then back, and finally got down on my hands and knees to see under an intervening branch. A subdued cackle reminded me that I was not alone. Two young women were coming along the path behind me. Startled and somewhat affronted, I walked on in a great hurry. But I returned later, by another route, and got one of the best nibbies in my collection.

On you go, quietly glancing about you. A blackbird screams a wild warning, a rabbit lobs away up to its burrow, or a pheasant rockets up with a volley of staccato rage, but otherwise you have the place to yourself, and one great consolation: your quarry has roots and may not elude you once you have spotted it.

Let us suppose that after, say, half-an-hour, when you are already a little cock-eyed with leering to right and left, and on the point of abandoning the whole foolish ploy, your eye suddenly alights on what appears to be the very nonpareil of nibbies.

Its stem, you observe, is straight, with a minimum of twigs and branches. It is of just about the correct thickness, not too supple, not too stolid. Its bark is cool-grey, smooth, and flawless. You pause a moment, in rapt contemplation, then whip out your trowel and go to work. To the beginner, the tyro of nibbie-stalking, an energetic and well-trained dog might seem an asset in this business of baring the roots. But I have not found it so. Dogs are inclined to become excited and, in their enthusiasm to scrape and spoil the soft bark of the roots. I tried a terrier once or twice during my first nibbying season, but this lack of finesse compelled me to abandon the dog in favour of the more laborious but less temperamental trowel. And to be truthful, the expression of frustration on the dog's face when he discovered that all I wanted were a few roots, became rather unnerving.

These are anxious moments for the keen nibbier, for everything depends on the shape of the roots. Yet the hand that wields the trowel must not tremble; the soil must be cleared away with a surgeon's skill. It is at this point that the reason for choosing a bank, rather than flat ground, becomes apparent. In such surroundings there is much more chance that the root will have the correct bend, which should be as nearly right-angled as possible. This is the real fascination of nibbying, for no two roots have the same shape, but there is an element of suspense as well, for it is at this stage that many an otherwise promising nibbie has come to naught. The root may be wrongly turned, have an insufficient angle, or may be divided, or be over-thick or thin. And in these cases, however excellent the stem may be, it is wise to replace the soil, sadly but firmly. This may occur several times during an afternoon's nibbying, but the keen sportsman treats it as a normal hazard of his hobby, and presses on in search of other game.

It may be late in the afternoon before you find a really good specimen. You are muddy, and rather tired, but, as always, a thrill warms your heart as, delicately, you clear away the last of the soil and the main root is laid bare: well-shaped, and with an interesting twirl towards the end, where the root has twisted to get round a stone. Quickly, for the light is fading, you unlimber your little saw and with swift judgement select the point for the amputation of the subsidiary roots. A delicate operation, this, for the bark is tender and the roots soft, and a false stroke or a hasty cut with the saw might result in splitting the root, and all your work would be in vain.

At last the roots are severed and carefully, for there may still be a hidden root to drag and split the head, you ease the plant from the ground. The next stage is to lop off the branches with a sharp knife, taking good care not to slice into the bark. The nibbie may now be inspected.

It is still in the rough, with quantities of soil adhering to it and the small hairy roots blurring its outlines, but its potentialities should at last be apparent. And, sided by a ready fancy, what a variety of shapes and forms these heads can take! – a trumpeting elephant a gargoyle, or some strange heraldic beast, a fierce-eyed bird of prey. The possibilities are endless. And when you get home, with a shameless appetite for company, a good cleaning under a cold tap will often reveal fresh touches of fantasy. But though the fingers may itch to trim up the head and accentuate the resemblances that imagination suggests, it is well to lay the nibbie aside for a while, to allow the soft root-bark to toughen and set hard. Then, many a happy hour may be spent, trimming and cleaning. By warming the stem at the fire, and pressing it against the knee, it is possible to straighten out slight bends. The last stage is reached when the nibbie is cut to the correct length and a ferrule fitted.

While there is little doubt that they provide the best all-round nibbies, the enthusiastic collector does not confine his attentions to ash-plants alone. To mention only two, there are hazel and rosewood nibbies well worth searching for. Hazel, with its ruddy, speckled bark, sometimes with a gleam of gold in it, yields many a fine nibbie, but as a rule the head has to be cut from the main root-mass, and this takes a deal of time and patience. Rosewood, too, is rewarding in colour, ranging from a fine glowing red in new wood, to a dull lizard green, but this is prickly work, and the stem is never as smooth as in the other varieties owing to the thorns.

Last of all, and matter for the purist, the nibbier by vocation, is sloe-wood or blackthorn, but only the fanatic will spend an entire afternoon creeping on all-fours through a thicket of black-thorn, his flesh pierced and his clothing ripped to shreds by its needles and stained by the green powdery lichen of its branches. Most of the blackthorn addicts I have known have suffered from deep-seated psychological disturbances, but whether this is cause or effect I should hesitate to say.

One final word; after a successful nibbie season, and many an evening's whittling and bending, you find that your hall-stand, already crammed with last year's crop, simply will not hold more than two out of the dozen you have finished. The question of disposal arises. This may seem easy: give the things away. But to do so is harder than it seems. You approach a friend, saying, "How would you like a good nibbie? I have one to spare." He looks at you without enthusiasm and replies, "Oh, thanks all the same, old man, but I have one that does me very well." The fool! He has <u>one</u>. One nibbie for spring, summer, autumn, and winter; for a short brisk walk or a long tramp in the hills, a gay jaunt or a bout of sombre striding – one nibbie!

You explain something of this to him. He is unconvinced, but rather than offend you, he accepts. Gradually, in this way the season's stock is disposed of. But what of the third season? You still have the first year's stock. The second year's you have given away to all your friends. What then? Well, I decided to do good by stealth. Whenever I called on anyone, I made a point of taking a nibbie with me, putting it in their hall-stand, and forgetting to take it away. With irritating honesty, some were returned, but the majority were kept.

This year will be my fourth nibbying season. Already, the question of disposal rears its ugly head. But little reck I! The leaves are twirling down. Every day sees more and more potential nibbies etched, as it were, against the sky. The hunt is up! And the slogan is "Fraxinus Excelsior!"

ODDS & ENDS

ANCIENT ENDEARMENT

"Oh, ee're juist ma little troot I the burn!"

Do we tack our pain
On to their claim for terrain.

The hamely porridge
Chief o' Scotia's food
That folk avoided
Whenever they could

BENEDICTUS ET ANATHEMA

Bless all railway junctions
In their northward functions.
Bless the cheery man in blue
Who shouts the sequence loud and true
Ending with Carlisle.
But afflict, oh Lord, with bile,
Rheums, fluxes, phlems and chyle,
The shambling ghoul whose drooling mouth
Mumbles at Crewe of stations south.

EPITAPHS

BOTHER

Aye, so hei's gotten away,
Auld Slack . . .
Weel, hei got throwt
Gey canny. But of coorse
Hei was aye bothert
Wi' his back.

COOK

Oh waes mei for
Puir Maggie Jane
And wad she still was leevin' . . .
I wadna swapt yin
O' her blackcurrant tairts
For a' the joys o' heevin!
A bairn cleaning door handles with brasso and a cloot –
"Is that better, Auntie Bella?"
"Aye, It's shinin' like a kittlin's ei."

FLICHTAN GEESE

Hech, sirs! The denty fowk!
Primpan by, pair by pair,
Kirkgaun,
Withoot e'en a gledge
At the craik and pen-whussle
O yon arra-heid o geese,
Straucht-craigit and shair,
I' the reid-rosie, the caller, the clear,
Sunset air!

MISTRESS SMITH

O Mistress Smith she has a bairn
She is a joyfu' wumman;
The steer she makes aboot the thing
Wad gar yin think it's human!

CHURCH PARADE

Apt is alliteration's artful aid
When blow the bungling bugles
of the Boys' Brigade.

THIRTY SIX HOURS

THIRTY-SIX HOURS

The Penguin New Writing No. 19, 1944
(translated into several foreign languages)

For a fortnight before the baby was due he had phoned on alternate nights. Then, as the date that the doctor had given slipped past in an anti-climax of fear and hope, he had made a nightly pilgrimage up the muddy paths from the dispersal lines, sometimes to queue in the windy December dark outside the kiosk while others rang and waited and hoped, other times to get straight into the box and put the call through and hear the clipped impersonal voices of operators as they passed him on, northward. The rain would beat on the panes and the searchlights grope and fence and stalk the sky on stilts of light and the coins in his hand grow sweaty and slippery as he gripped them in his anxiety for news.

Then at last he would be told to insert the money. Fumbling in the dark, the coins would clang into the box and his wife's voice would come over the wire small and clear, a little breathless and frightened, so that tears would prickle his eyes and he longed to dash open the door and rush through the night to comfort her and help her to bear the pain that was so near.

Instead, they would talk trivialities and there were long seconds of silence in which they were both tongue-tied by strangeness of what lay before them. Then both would start nervously to speak at the same time; the tension would relax and they would laugh and start again. Till in what seemed no time at all the operator's voice would break curtly in (had she been listening all the time?) and he would say, in defiance of all operators, 'I love you, honey,' and sweet and small would have his answer and wait a moment, even though the line had gone dead, before stumbling forth again into the rain, back to the hut and the friendly, half-ribald inquiries of his mates.

The night before last, however, had been different. He had got straight into the kiosk and the call had gone through almost at once. In the few seconds wait before the home exchange gave him the number, panic gripped him. It was bitterly cold and windy, with a wild, tangled cloud-wrack flying across the sky, revealing at odd moments a glimpse of the moon's brilliant, untroubled face. It was during one of these brief intervals of light that he suddenly became aware of his face staring at him from the mirror, and somehow his reflected eyes told him what his brain did not yet know.

And it was not his wife's voice but a friendly neighbour's that he heard.

'Is that you, Danny? Oh, I've got good news for you tonight! Mary was taken away to the home this morning. Yes, she is alright. They phoned to-night and everything is going well.'

'When will they know?' He heard his voice, barking and hoarse and angrily abrupt. 'When will there be news?'

'There should be news in the morning,' the soothing voice went on, 'ring up about nine. I'm sure we'll know by then. It's no use ringing up later to-night, it's nearly ten now, and you must wait till morning and have as much patience as you can, Danny. Now, don't you worry!'

'Alright, I'll ring up again in the morning.' After the first shock he felt quieter and more docile. The woman was experienced, she had a family of her own and knew more of such matters than he. 'I'll ring up about nine,' he said. 'Goodnight. Are you sure that you'll know then?'

'Yes, I think there will be news for you in the morning – and, oh, how proud you'll be! Now go to bed, laddie, and try not to worry. Goodnight!'

'Goodnight!' he had said, feeling stupid and tired as he laid down the receiver. So it had happened at last – was happening, anyway. He dared not think what *was* happening. 'Proud you'll be,' she had said. How in hell's name could anyone feel proud?

I'll never sleep, he had thought, as he slid down between his blankets a quarter of an hour later. I'll never sleep. But before the vicious circle of wondering and hoping and fearing could start, and the moments of sheer unbelief that such a thing was happening to *them*, he had fallen into a heavy sleep which lasted till nearly half-past six the following morning.

As he slowly awakened he had known that he was worried, terribly worried, before he remembered the events of the previous night. Then a great flood of guilty shame overwhelmed him. He had slept, actually *slept*, like a callous hog, while she was going through agony. He swore at himself under his breath as he hurried, blear-eyed, up the path to the cook-house. Sleeping!

He drank some tea and ate a piece of bread and margarine, and went back to the hut to wait till nine. His mates left him alone. They were, in fact, embarrassed. They spoke to him as one by one and in scrambling groups they hurried off to parade. This was an unusual situation; unfamiliar emotions were involved. Their words were rough and kindly, but he did not hear them. He had forgotten all about work and nobody reminded him. He simply sat on the edge of his bed, smoking cigarette after cigarette and glancing at his watch every few minutes as the frowsy morning light of winter crept slowly into the hut.

At last it was time to go to the phone. He had to force himself to lift the receiver. When he got through, he immediately suspected the brightness of the neighbour's voice. With her first word he knew that there was still no news.

Desperately afraid, he argued and blustered, but it was no use. The woman kept repeating that everything was going normally, that nature was taking its course, that he mustn't worry. The idiocy of this well-meaning advice nearly made him lose control of himself altogether, but somehow he managed to maintain civility. He arranged to ring up again after tea.

The day went past somehow, in a trance of worry that rose at times to unbearable poignancy so that he had to leave what he was doing and slip away to pace up and down and smoke. Then it would die away to dullness again. And then, once more, he was in the kiosk, and surely, surely, in God's name, there must be an end to this, now - now!

The worried voice came over the wire: tired now, and no longer bright with easy hope.

'Still no news, Danny. Oh, I'm sorry, but there's still no news!'

'But, woman, it can't go on like this. There must be news. There must be!' He felt himself bawling into the phone. He dug his nails into the hard shiny vulcanite.

'I'm sorry, but we rang up half an hour ago and they said that there was still no news. Can you ring up again later? There must be news soon.'

'Yes, yes, I'll ring up again. In an hour if I can get through. But surely there should be news by now. It can't go on as long as this – what can be wrong? It doesn't take all this time.'

'Now, Danny, things like this *can* take a long time. Remember, it's her first baby. You'll have to hang on, somehow. We are all hanging on. Ring up again in an hour.'

He walked in the dark along the rough country road till his watch told him half an hour had gone past, then turned and half-walked, half-ran back in case he should be late.

After a twenty-minute wait outside, during which some imbecile babbled into the phone about a pair of drawers that were missing from a parcel of washing, he got into the kiosk. The line was very busy, the operator explained, but she would try. She tried for half an hour. He shifted and smoked and fidgeted and swapped the receiver from left ear to right and back again. The trees outside waved their skeleton branches soundlessly and moonlight shone lividly on the ruffled puddles of the road.

The operator apologised from time to time, startling him from the feverish day-dream into which he had relapsed, but it was no use; finally she told him that there was no hope of his getting through till some impossibly late hour, and no certainty even of that. He could not think of disturbing the neighbour when she was certain to have gone to bed. She had been troubled enough already with his affairs. Slowly he laid down the receiver. It was hopeless. He went back to the hut and to bed.

He slept fitfully during the night and awoke in a mood of numb despair. He felt that his wife had sailed away on seas of pain and danger far beyond his knowledge. His capacity for worry seemed exhausted for the time being, and a cowardice he was too tired to fight began to take possession of him. He dared not go to the phone. Instead he went straight down to the hangar. They were bound to wire as soon as there was news, he thought. They had arranged it that way, months ago. Whatever had happened, he would know soon, and he would not invite the blow; he would wait as calmly as he might for its inevitable fall.

Opening his tool-box, he put on his overalls and selected a few tools. The job he had to do was awkward and tiring, but he had volunteered for it as a means of achieving at least temporary forgetfulness. It involved crawling down through the fuselage of the fighter he was servicing and emerging, when the job was done, through an aperture near the tail to save the terribly awkward process of crawling feet first back to the cockpit. The fuselage could be entered by the aperture, which measured about fourteen inches by twelve, but once in, it was almost impossible for a man of more than very slight build to manoeuvre his legs and body into the position necessary to do the job on the tail-strut shock-absorbing gear.

He climbed up the main plane and swung himself into the cockpit. The seat had been removed, so, stowing the tools in his pockets, he crouched on all-fours, pushed his head and shoulders through into the fuselage and started to lever himself along by gripping the rudder and elevator control cables.

Soon his whole body was stretched prone on the taut wires. Like being on a gridiron, he thought. . who was that bloke who was roasted on a gridiron? Some saint or other. I wonder what has happened, when the wire will come . . .

From some recess of his subconscious, a speech from *The Gondoliers* started to reel off like a crazy ticker-tape: ' . . . This is the ducal Palace, and it is here that the Grand Inquisitor resides. As a Castilian hidalgo of ninety-five quarterings, I regret that I am unable to pay my state visit on a horse . . . . something . . . . something . . . . an unusually wet season . . . equestrian exercise is impracticable . . .'

Slowly he eased himself along towards the small lamp he had placed ready at the rear. The hangar was poorly lit at the best of times, but during the overcast December days the inside of the fuselage was very dark. The well was dirty and sticky with glycol; he could smell it faintly as he rested for a moment, breathless.

She cannot be dead, he thought, she cannot be; she is too alive, too full of loving-kindness. In Suffolk, when she came to stay last year in May, we used to wander the lanes at night. She wanted to have a walking-stick, so we walked and walked, examining all the young ash trees in the hedges, but in the end we decided on a lovely hazel branch, speckled and ruddy. I cut it carefully and we sat down on the grassy hedge-bank among the red campion and tiny geranium flowers, and she watched intently as I trimmed and cut her initials on it. After that, she carried the stick always when we went walking.

On her last evening, after our last walk, she climbed over the churchyard wall and laid it carefully down in the lee of a tilted lichened tombstone. 'Stay there till I come back,' she had whispered, between sadness and happiness. And whenever he had passed by the little grey village church after she had gone home, he had stopped to peep over the wall. It was still there, and when she came back in August, though the grass had been scythed in the interval, she had found it at once. It stood at home now, a symbol of their happiness; she had carried it all the way back with her at the summer's end . . .
The cables bit through his overalls, bruising his skin as he hitched and heaved himself forward again, working himself inch by inch through the narrow dark fuselage. When he reached about half-way there began the awkward business of getting past the flare-chute and radio equipment. He had to lie on his left side to do this; the space was too narrow to allow the width of both shoulders. Slowly, sweating in the smelly gloom, he

edged past. The fuselage tapered here and the space grew smaller. Cables kept catching at his hair. He relaxed for a few moments.

Outside, he could hear his mates chatting and laughing as they worked. He was suddenly angry that they could be so unconcerned as to laugh at a time like this. Then he remembered how casual had been his own interest last year when one of them had been in the same situation; he had merely felt vaguely sorry for the bloke, had shaken hands with him when the good news came through, and had promptly forgotten all about it as soon as the fellow had left the hangar. You worked with people, smoked and laughed and drank with them, but your life and theirs never really merged at all in any more than the shallow comradeship that arises from sharing the vicissitudes of duties, work and weather. All their real thoughts were centred on home. On leave, in real life, this existence was only a distant nightmare. He suddenly remembered his escape for forty-eight hours' leave after his first six weeks' training.

It was in the autumn, two years ago, and he had arranged to meet Mary at a railway junction about half-way between home and his camp. His train had been nearly two hours late, but there was no sign at all of the train from the north on which she was travelling. He had hung about for nearly two hours watching the line, peering beyond the dim lights of the platform into the murky black-out. Soldiers sat on the forms, huddled in dejection, waiting for trains they had probably no desire to catch. A few had given up hope altogether and had curled up in corners to sleep. Occasionally a train, fantastically late by ordinary standards, would draw in at one of the platforms, releasing a hurrying wave of people that receded as quickly as it had risen, leaving a few more forlorn souls high and dry. But there had been no sign at all of the only train he was interested in, and at last he had given up and gone miserably to the hotel where he had booked a room.

The night porter had let him in and shown him to their room. Wearily, still clinging to the last shreds of hope that she might turn up, he began to prepare for bed. He was brushing his teeth when he heard footsteps approaching along the corridor. A tap on the door, it opened, and there she had stood, rosy, bright-eyed, already soothing away in her eager, gentle solicitude the harsh novelty of having become a number. She had come to him through blitz and black-out. It was, he still thought, the happiest moment of his whole life.

And next day, in the golden, tenuous October sunlight, they had sat on a bench in the market-place among the mufflered, bleary old men who inhabit such places, holding hands, smiling into one another's eyes in the silliest way, absurdly happy merely to be sitting side by side . . . .

And now these days were gone, gone maybe for ever. If only he could know what had happened. He could bear even the worst news better than this dragging pain of suspense and foreboding.

A twinge of cramp warned him that he must go forward again. He pulled along the cables; only another few feet to go. His chest was sore and he was sticky with glycol and his hands felt raw and strained.

'Go for the mail, Fred!' he heard someone shout, 'It's nearly a quarter past ten.'

'Okay!' came the reply, and shortly afterwards the creak and rattle of the knockabout bicycle leaving the hanger.

He had reached the tail-strut at last. As he groped and wriggled to get his tools from his pockets and stretched to reach the job, he wondered if the wire could possibly come along with the mail. Oh, it couldn't be much longer now! Surely they would send it straight along from Signals as soon as it came in. If it lasted any longer, he'd have to go to the phone.

Steadying himself, he started to remove a split-pin. The lamp was a damned nuisance, it never seemed to be in the right place. He peered forward, his eyes smarting, trying to straighten the legs of the pin and draw it out with pliers. At last he got it out and reached forward again with a spanner.

Suddenly he heard shouting, shouting that drew rapidly nearer, and the clatter of the old bicycle being ridden furiously up the hanger.

'Danny! Danny!' he heard Fred's voice and the crash as the bicycle was dropped hastily on the floor. 'Danny! Wire, wire, come on, get out – quick!'

A hand, wagging an orange envelope, suddenly appeared in the aperture. A cold terror seized him. He reached to grab the telegram. It was just beyond reach, and he tried to stretch a little farther. The muscles of his calves sharply contracted into an agonising knot. Involuntarily he relaxed, but the cramps kept its grip. He could not take hold of the telegram.

'Come on, Danny, for God's sake!' cried Fred. The hand waggled the envelope impatiently. 'Don't you want to read the bloody thing?'

'Cramp, cramp; get me out quick!' he managed to whisper.

'What?' said the voice stupidly. 'What's the matter?'

'Cramp, you dimwit, cramp! Get me out, quick!' He yelled as the pain grew worse. The fuselage seemed to be closing in on him, growing tighter and darker. Reason left him, and he began to struggle wildly to get back a couple of feet and get his head out through the aperture. The telegram was forgotten in the madness of pain. With a frantic effort he managed to get his head and one shoulder clear. Fred had realised at last what was the matter and was trying to help him out and shouting to the others to give a hand. They came running as the agony became unbearable. He blacked-out.

When he came to they had hauled him out somehow, and Bert, the ex-policeman, was massaging his legs.

'Equestrian exercise impracticable . . .' he muttered. Then he realised what had happened. He looked down at himself. He was bruised and sore all over, his overalls were torn, and there was blood on his hands. Sweating and breathless after heaving his twelve stones out of the fuselage, his mates regarded him with concern.

'There, Danny,' said Bert at last, 'feel better now?'

'Yes, yes, I'll be okay now,' he grunted, struggling to his feet. 'Bloody silly of me to get cramp like that – and then to faint. Never did that before.'

He looked on the hanger floor. The telegram lay in a pool of oil close to his feet. Someone had trampled on it as they had hauled him out. He stooped to pick it up.

Before he opened it he glanced round at his mates. They were silent, standing in a half-circle watching the envelope in his hand. He tried to smile, then suddenly, impatiently, he tore the envelope open and unfolded the wire. It was soaked in oil, translucent as a fish-and-chip paper. He had to hold it up to the light to read it.

'Your daughter born last night nine o'clock. Both well,' it said. He repeated the words slowly aloud, with the same heavy emphasis on each word as though the message were meaningless. Then suddenly he yelled: 'Oi, oi, lads, I've got a daughter – a daughter!'

They crowded him then, slapping his back, shaking his hand, telling him to get cracking along to the orderly-room and get his pass signed and off home. He walked away up the hangar, their congratulations still in his ears, elated, stepping quickly and confidently.

But after he had gone a little way and was out of earshot his pace gradually slowed. He began to think of the telegram again. Nine o'clock last night the baby was born. Both well. Nine o'clock last night – thirty-six hours after she had been taken away. It had lasted through a whole day and a night and the whole of another day . . . both well . . .

Suddenly, in a flash of revelation, he realised the terror and drawn-out agony implicit in the bald statement of the telegram. Without thinking what he was doing, he broke into a shambling run. Tears blinded him, and trying to blink them away he stumbled and almost fell up the shallow wooden steps into the office.

SHORT STORIES

BRITISH BROADCASTING CORPORATION

A MATTER OF TIME

A short story by David Hill

Read by Harold Wightman (BBC recording)

Time signals, and Big Ben, and a grandfather clock.
These were Aitken Sharp's obsession – until his wife's untimely death.

RECORDING:	**Wednesday, 11th May, 8.15 – 8.45pm**
REHEARSAL:	**From 7.30pm**
STUDIO:	**Glasgow 10**
R.P. Ref.No:	**DGW 26608**
PRODUCER:	**Roderick MacLean**
TRANSMISSION:	**Tuesday, 31st May, 10.15-10.30pm SHS**

A MATTER OF TIME

READER:

Aye, it's a fine grandfaither clock, sir. A fine auld clock. Solid oak case, and a handsome pentin o Tam o Shanter and Souter Johnnie abune the dial. It's been tickin awa there withoot a stop, the five years I've had it in my shop. Ever since I retired frae the Police Force and began this wee bit business wi antiques and sic-like.

Is it for sale? Weel . . . . no, sir. I couldna sell it. For sentimental reasons, as ye micht say. It has a history, that clock. Quite a history. Wad ye like to hear it? What's that? Och, no . . . . I'm in nae hurry, sir. It's wearin on past shuttin-time, I ken. But in this line o business we're no' slappin punds o margarine across the counter a' day and skelpin up the shutters on the chap o six. And when I get haud o somebody like yoursel that's interested in auld nick-nacks weel . . . . I juist let time gang on a loose rein. Plenty o time. A' the time i' the world . . . . Aye, time . . . . It's a queer thing, time. It gets owre muckle attention, nooadays, I whiles think. Everything maun be dune to the verra meenit. A job is valued for the time it takes, now. No' the work that's put intill't. And in my opeenion, the wireless is a lot to blame, wi a' yon time-signals and Big Ben and the like. In my young days, we were mair casual aboot time. If a clock was inclined to gang slow, weel, ye juist put up wi't and made allowance for it, the same as ye hae to dae wi some folk. And if it gaed fast . . . weel, ye'd time for a wee bit smoke. But a' this deadly Greenwich accuracy . . . . a' thir pips, and London clocks gaun off like guns in your lug . . . . ye've nae chance. They've gotten Auld Faither Time fair sergeant-majored, wi his heuk at the slope, and leggin oot like a recruit insteed o bein treated wi the respect that's due to his douce auld age. Aye, this pippin and boomin on the wireless are a kind o mixed blessin, and wi some folk they can lead to a fair obsession wi time. Ye'll see what I mean, sir, when I tell ye aboot the man that yince owned yon grandfaither clock.

Aitken Sharp, his name was. Aye. He had the chemist's shop i' the toon, here. And if ever there was a man that got to be fair hag-ridden wi time, it was him. He was oot o his bed at the seven o'clock pips, and sittin doon to his breakfast at the echt o'clock pips, and at a quarter to nine, on the dot, he was shuttin the gate o his bit bungalow up on the ootskirts o the toon, near the by-pass . . . Then, wi a quick look at his watch, in case o ony jookery-packery, he was off doon the road to his shop, wi his heid cockit off at the side . . . . listenin . . . listenin a' the time. Listening for what? I whiles wondered . . . .

At twa meenits to nine, he was in at the back door o his shop, and on wi the wireless in his dispensary, and slap, bang, the bolts were drawn as Big Ben was striking.

Yin o'clock, and he was nippin up the steps to set the shop clock to richts, in case it had played the foumart wi him durin' the forenoon, then slap wi the bolt, and off for his denner. Aye. And the same at six o'clock – and richt nippy he wad be wi a customer that cam wanderin in late wi a prescription.

He was the same at hame. It used to tickle me, when I was on nicht-shift. I wad pass his bungalow awa on the edge o the toon at the end o my beat, aye aboot eleven o'clock. And I wad see the lichts o each room snap on . . . . then off. The next room . . . on, then off, as he gaed roond, checkin the clocks.

His shop had belonged to his wife's faither when I was a laddie, and Sharp had come as an assistant when the auld man had begun to fail. And there was Madge, the auld man's dochter, fat and forty, man-less and nane owre gleg. And there was Sharp, twenty-five, wi his way to make. Weel, he mairriet her, and in a year or twa the auld man died, leavin a' thing to his yin dochter. And we watched, as the years gaed creepin by, we watched Sharp slowly turn frae a smert-like young man into yon dried-up fidget o a thing, aye listening . . . .

Weel, his wife took some kind of paralytic stroke when she was in her late fifties and Sharp no' muckle owre forty, and they moved into their bungalow so that she could be the easier handled frae sofa and wheel-chair to bed. And I can aye mind havin to knock Sharp up, late yin simmer nicht, to get some medicine for a sick bairn. It was juist on eleven o'clock. Their licht was switched on, but the curtains werena drawn, and as I stude there, wi my thumb ready to press the bell, I could see Sharp at the bedside, lookin doon at his wife, wi his heid cockit off at the side . . . . listenin . . . . listenin to what . . . .? Listening, I thocht as I stude there, listenin to his life tickin awa, and wonderin, maybe, as he lookit doon at the puir wumman wi yon silly smile on her face, puir thing, wonderin, maybe, if he'd sellt his short bit tairm o time owre cheap, for the sake o a wee bit security . . . . and was beginning sairly to grudge and rue the bargain he'd made . . . . But the pips soondit frae the wireless at the bedside, and Sharp looked up at the clock. The spell was broken. I rang the bell.

Aweel . . . . fower or five months efter that, I was juist gaun off duty at the Police Station, when a phone-call came through frae Edinburgh. It was Sharp the chemist. It was early-closing day, and a dirty foggy yin at that, and he'd gane off to the city to get supply o some drug he'd run short o, but he'd been unlucky. The firm was oot o stock and as we're near enough half-way atween the twa cities, he was gaun on to Glasgow to try his luck. He thocht, wi the fog, he'd better bide the nicht there, and wad I be guid enough to ask the District Nurse, as a special favour, to look in aboot nine o'clock and see that Mrs Sharp was got into bed and settled for the nicht, and he was be back as airly as he could, the next day?

Weel, I ca'd on the Nurse on my way hame, and she promised to look in, and I thocht nae mair aboot it till the next morning when I cam on duty and fund a fine auld stramash gaun on.

The daily wumman had arrived at Sharp's hoose as usual, at echt in the morning, and fund the wireless blarin awa, and Mrs Sharp deid in her bed. The doctor had been ca'd in, and he had said that she appeared to have died frae an overdose o the sleepin-tablets that were kept at her bedside. Then the Nurse had been summoned, and she said that she had given Mrs Sharp the normal dose o tablets, and left the hoose at nine. She was certain o the time, she said, for Big Ben had come on the wireless as she shut the bedroom door, and the grandfaither clock . . . . aye, yon clock, sir, had struck the hour as she left the hoose. So there was naething could be done till Sharp came back frae Glasgow, and I was sent alang to wait aboot the place and hear what he had to say.

Aye, weel, it would be nearly half-past ten when his wee car cam doon the quiet lane frae the by-pass and drew up at the door, and I steppit forrit to gie him the sad news. He took it verra quietly, and askit me to come wi him into the hoose.

It was daithly still, in there. The only soond was the steedy tickin o the grandfaither clock i' the hall. Sharp lookit at the clock. "She is beyond time now" he said. "Aye, she is that, puir thing," I said. "But she was an ailin wumman . . . . " "Aye, that's so," he said. "That's so." He gaed into the bedroom, and I stude waitin, lookin at the clock. Man, there was something kind o hypnotic aboot its slow, solemn tick-tock . . . . tick-tock. I fair had to gie myself a shake when he cam oot. "Now, Mr Sharp," I said, "I'll need to get a bit statement frae ye . . . . "

Weel, there was naething strange aboot his movements. He'd left Edinburgh the back o nine, efter a meal wi a freend o his in the same line o business, and he'd booked in at his hotel in Glasgow shortly efter eleven-thirty. He'd ta'en a guid bit time on the road, richt enough, but it was a dirty foggy nicht, and he'd had trouble wi a flat tyre as weel. I had a fly look at his spare wheel later. It was punctured richt enough, so there was naething we could really make a fuss aboot. Nae other evidence cropped up, and i' the hinder end it was juist concluded that his wife had ta'en the tablets herself, for her ain reasons . . . . and little enough she had to leeve for, puir body.

But efter the enquiry was a' feenished and bye-wi, Sharp never seemed to settle doon again. So it was nae surprise, in a way, when he announced that he'd sellt what was now his ain business and the hoose, and was leavin the district. He sellt a'thing, every stick. And that's how I got the clock, sir. A tame enough feenish to a story, maybe, but I'd fair ta'en a fancy for the clock, and I bocht it at the sale. I got it reasonable . . . . verra reasonable, and a guid-gaun clock it is. Aye, Sharp gaed awa to leeve up on yin o the Hebridean islands. I forget its name, juist for the meenit. Someplace richt off the map, as ye micht say. He bocht a wee cottage, and, man, there was somebody up there on holiday frae hereabouts last year, met him there. A fair beachcomber he'd turned, seeminly, fishin and loafin his life awa. No' a clock in his hoose, they said. And when they askit him the time o day, he clawed his heid, then said he thocht it was Thursday! Aye, a changed man . . . . .a changed man.

What's that? Is my clock an echt-day or a thirty-hour movement? Weel, that's the yin snag wi't. It's a thirty-hour. Aye. It needs windin every nicht, ye may say, to keep it gaun . . . . Eh? Certainly the clock was gaun, when Sharp cam back frae Glasgow. Did I no' tell ye that I stude and lookit at it, and heard it tickin awa there? How did it come to be gaun, ye say, and him awa the nicht afore ? . . . . Oh . . .. . Now that's fair a bit problem, sir. It is that. It kinda seems to indicate something that wants lookin into, as ye micht say. Aye. Time's a queer thing. And so is a twenty-year auld habit . . . .

Mebbe we could shut the shop noo, sir, and you and me could hae a dauner roond by the Station and hae a wee word wi the Inspector. Aye. That's it. A wee word wi the Inspector.

BRITISH BROADCASTING CORPORATION

MORNING STORY from Scotland

"TOO HOT FOR CANDLES"

A short story by David Hill

Read by Douglas Murchie

TRANSMISSION:	**Friday, 18th May, 1956 11.15-11.30am. Light Programme**
REHEARSAL:	**From 10.15am**
STUDIO:	**Glasgow No. 8**
PRODUCER:	**Roderick MacLean**

READER:

Of course there was never any real need for me to work at all. My wife's money would have kept both of us in comfort. But I could never get her to part with it. Not a penny piece. I didn't mind so much, as long as my business kept going. It gave me a little bit of independence. Then the day came when the bank manager shook his head and said that they couldn't allow me any more credit. I knew then that I was at her mercy.

It didn't take her long to let me know, either. I had held off as long as I could, but after weeks without a drink or a smoke, I just couldn't stand it any longer. I asked her for some money.

"Money!" she said, in the sneering voice I had hated for so long. "Money! You married me, you good for nothing boozer, hoping to get your hands on my money. But I was too smart for you. And where would it be, now, if you had? In the tills of half the pubs and bookies in the town, no doubt. Still, you'll have to keep up appearances somehow, I suppose. You can have five shillings a week."

"Five bob!" I said.

"Five bob. And you'll have to earn it. You'll take Fluff-fluff for a walk, every day. He hasn't been at all well, poor soul, and the vet says he needs regular exercise. I can't take him myself, the way my heart is. But it'll be good for you. Give these great flapping feet of yours something to do."

It was the first time she had ever referred to my feet. And that reference – and the insult of the five shilling pittance – decided something I had been weighing-up for quite a while. She would have to be . . . . eliminated from my life.

You see, I have big feet. Very big. I have to get my shoes specially made. And I'm sensitive about my feet. I always have been. They used to shout after me at school . . . "Yah . . . . Big Feet . . . . Plates o' Meat . . . . Big Feet . . . ." The little swine . . . . And when I meet people in the street – strangers – their eyes have a way of travelling downwards to my feet, and they go past with a hateful smirk on their ugly faces.

My little black figure had big feet too. That was what drew me to it when I first saw it in the window of a junkshop, one day when I was out with darling Fluff-fluff, earning my five bob. It was some sort of Eastern image, about eight or nine inches high, and the feet were big and wedge-shaped, not separate, carved in one piece. It stood in a sort of half-crouching position, the face still, thick-lipped, waiting . . . . I used to pass the shop every day with that fat pampered dog wheezing along at my side, and always the figure was there, crouched on the big feet . . . . waiting . . . . Then one day I went in. The old man who kept the shop came forward.

"That's an interesting figure you have in the window."

"Oh, yes, sir. That's a piece of primitive art, that is. Worth a lot of money in the right quarter."

He lifted it out of the window and set it on the counter. "Nice and steady on its feet," he said. "Should be. They're big enough . . ." and I saw his eyes glancing down.

"How much?"

"Oh . . . . Gimme five bob. Alright? I'm giving it away . . . ."

"Wrap it up." I said.

There was a scene when I took it home. She peered at it with those mean bulging eyes of hers, so like her blasted dog's. "What's this hideous rubbish? How much did you pay for it?"

"Five shillings."

"Five shillings of my good money for an evil-looking thing like that! You're not keeping it in the house! Enough to give anybody the creeps. Take it away to your tool-shed where you smoke your filthy pipe. It'll be company for you. You're a pair . . . ." And I saw her squinting from its feet to mine. I said nothing. I was beginning to learn from the figure already. It waited, crouching, with a blank, still face. I learnt to do the same . . . . to wait. My chance would come.

A week or two later, I was tidying-up the tool shed, when I noticed that my little figure was getting a bit dusty. There was a rainwater barrel outside, so I popped it in. it floated alright. I went back into the shed for a duster. When I came out, it struck me that there was something strange about the way it was floating . . . feet uppermost. Surely, I thought, feet like that should be the heaviest part of it . . . I fished it out and dried it, pondering a bit. Then I got a pencil and began tapping it . . the head, arms, body, legs. They all sounded the same. Only the feet were different. They had almost a hollow sound. I began to get excited. I knew then that the figure had been sent to me . . . .sent for a purpose.

I soon found what I was looking for. A small circle on the sole of the feet, half-hidden by dirt and grime. I scraped at it with a pocket-knife. It was some sort of waxy substance. I dug into it, and the little plug fell out, and a heap of greyish-brown powder came dribbling out of the hollow feet into my hand. About as much as the ash of two or three cigarettes. I stood there for a long time, looking at it. I never had a moment's doubt that it was some kind of poison. Why else would it have been sent to me?

Of course I daren't take it to be analysed. That would have been fatal. All I could do was to experiment, to devise ways and means, and hope for the best. My wife had heart trouble, I knew. What could be simpler than to add some of the powder to her medicine? But I came up against a snag, there. No matter what I did, or how much I stirred, I couldn't get the powder to dissolve. So there was no use putting it in her medicine. It would just sink to the bottom and be found there when . . . . something had happened. I began to think I was beaten. Then, suddenly, she delivered herself into my hands! I had come in from taking her darling doggie for his walk.

"The doctor's been in," she said. "He's given me a strong heart medicine. Take the prescription round to the chemist's. Oh . . . . and get me some Gregory's Mixture as well."

"But it's only a week or so since you got the last lot."

"Well. What of it? I have to take it every morning. Go on, man. What are you mooning there for?"

Gregory's Mixture. You know the stuff. Excellent for its purpose, of course, but gritty . . . sandy . . . The very thing I was looking for. I bought two boxes, gave one to her, and put the other one in the tool shed. So far, so good.

Now I had to get out of the way for a few weeks. While I was still in business, I had consulted a specialist about my feet – they were giving me a good deal of trouble at the time. I'd had an x-ray, and was advised to have an operation. This would have meant being laid-up for a month or six weeks, and I just couldn't afford the time, then. It was different now. I went back to the specialist and told him that I was in constant pain and would like to have the operation performed as soon as possible. It was too easy. He rang up the hospital, and the whole thing was fixed up for the following week.

When the day came, I checked up on the amount of Gregory my wife had taken out of her box. Then I spent a little time in the tool shed. I used about half the powder, and carefully ran the remainder back into the hollow feet. Then I sealed up the hole with candle-grease, smoothed it off, and brought it round to the colour of the wood with a little black-lead. It was a perfect job. You couldn't see a thing. I turned at the door and looked at the figure on the shelf. It seemed to be watching me, and it looked lost and lonely. I couldn't leave it there. I hadn't the heart. So I popped it in my pocket, went up to the house, quietly exchanged the boxes of Gregory and set off for the hospital.

Well, the operation passed off alright. I was very comfortable there. I had a nice ward to myself, snug and warm, with the little black figure for company, on the shelf above the radiator. A week went past. Then another week. I began to wonder . . . . Three weeks . . . . Then one day my wife's doctor came into the ward. He looked grave. "I thought I'd better tell you," he said. "Your wife has become seriously ill. Her heart condition is much worse."

"Anything I can do?" I said, trying to keep calm.

He shook his head. "I doubt if she'll last more than a few days, poor woman. It's a great pity you're laid-up. But I'll keep you informed.

It was working out perfectly. Far better than my wildest hopes. It was only a questior of time, now . . . . of waiting a little longer . . . .

Three days later, the doctor came in again. "I'm sorry," he said. "It's all over , I'n afraid. Your wife had another severe attack last night. She died early this morning."

"Thank you for letting me know personally, doctor."

"Not at all. As little as I could do in the circumstances."

We discussed one or two matters relating to my wife's affairs. "I suppose I'll be hearing from her lawyers," I said.

He looked at me strangely. "As a matter of fact, there's something I have to tell you or that subject. When your wife became very ill, she made a new will. She asked me to tel you its contents. She has gifted her house as a Dogs Home and endowed it with all her money except £500, the interest on which will be yours during your lifetime. I think she said it was invested at 2½ per cent."

"Why . . . . the . . . .! that's . . .. five shillings a week."

"Near enough," he said.

" . . . .I'll ask the . . . .Welfare Officer to pop in and see you one of these days," he said "He'll be able to get you fixed up with a job, once you're fit again. You're comfortable enough in the meantime – snug quarters, eh? Next to the radiator. Hello – what's this you have on the shelf, here? It's a long time since I saw one of those."

He was looking at the little black figure.

"I was a ship's doctor in my young days," he said. "And I remember a time when there was quite a deal of trouble with some little figures just like that. A gang was using them for smuggling dope – opium mostly – but other things as well – poisons, even. The feet were hollow, you see."

He picked up the figure. "Uh-huh!" he said. "What's this?"

I looked – crawling with fear. On the spot where the figure had been standing, there was a little blob of candle-grease. A trickle of greyish-brown powder was running into his hand.

"Hum . . . interesting . . ." he said, walking over to the window. "Greyish-brown in colour, quite heavy . . ." then he went across the ward to the fireplace and blew a little of the powder into the fire. There was a shower of bright little sparks.

"Thought so," he said, dusting his hands. He set the figure back on the shelf. "Well . . . must be getting along . . . ."

As he pulled open the door, something made me look at the little black figure. It was swaying on its feet. I leapt to catch it, but before I was clear of the bed, it had crashed to the floor. The doctor looked at me with a curious expression on his face as I stood there, sick and weaving.

"A bit rocky on the feet, eh? Pretty unstable type . . . the figure, I mean . . . of course. It must have needed that stuff to steady it after the original contents were taken out. Fooled me for a moment, till I remembered that *they* used to use a wooden plug. Too hot for candles, where that fella came from originally, I daresay . . . ."

"What . . .was . . .the . . .powder . . .then?"

"Oh, just some fine iron filings . . .fairly heavy, you know . .. .Well . .. . .Goodbye."

BRITISH BROADCASTING CORPORATION

CENTENARY

A short story by David Hill

Read by Bryden Murdoch

RECORDING:	**Tuesday, 1st March, 12 noon-12.30pm**
REHEARSAL:	**From 11am**
STUDIO:	**Glasgow 10**
PRODUCER:	**Roderick MacLean**
R.P.Ref.No:	**DGW 26080**
TRANSMISSION:	**Sunday, 6th March, 10.35 -10.52pm approx.**
	Scottish Home Service

READER:

The shabby little second-hand bookshop was still there in the back-street on the way to the station. I looked at my watch. There was just time for a quick look at the penny box. It was the sixpenny box, nowadays, but "Ministers of the Disruption" and "The Terrier in Sport and Show Ring" still led a dusty weather-beaten life. It had to be something quick. So I settled for a scruffy little book of verse called "Starcleuch Edge", hurled my sixpence at the old man, and ran for my train.

I tried to read a paper for the first ten minutes of my journey, but the wheels of the train began to clatter "Starcleuch Edge . . . . Starcleuch Edge . . . ." so insistently, that I had to get the little book out. "Starcleuch Edge", by John Caverton. Printed for the author by William Sudden and Son, "Border Sentinel" Office, 1896. And there was John Caverton himself, glowering in side-whiskers from the frontispiece, defying the gentle reader to read.

1896 – just inside the vintage quarter-century for bardies. God bless them all, and their sonsy, flat-footed muse, I thought, as I turned the pages of lean spidery type and scratchy ornamented capitals. I had rescued dozens of them from penny boxes in my time. But this one seemed a bit different. There was no belly-crawling dedication to some laird who had promised to take a dozen copies. There was no patronising preface. Just the verses, in strong-standing Scots – un-pawky, hale and sound – and all on one theme. A hill called Starcleuch Edge.

First of all, it was boyhood hill, with racing cloud-shadows and blaeberries and the crying of whaups. Then a young man's hill, with rabbits to snare, and trout in the burns. And then a lover's hill, and the courting of a lass in the heathery howe. It was always a shepherd's hill: blithe with lambs, merry with whistling and the racing of collies at the clipping. The man seemed to see all life in relation to his hill.

Later, it became a bleak hateful hill, arrowed with sleet and rain, desolate with a heart loneliness. And at the last, both as a final reality and a refuge, it was an indifferent hill, aloof from both love and hate and fear and death – a symbol, only, of the earth's endurance and man's impermanence.

The early verses were stilted and conventional. The less said about the rather fulsome love-poems the better. But there was a crude power about the later verses; a tormented grappling with ideas he could hardly clothe in words. There were flaws, of course, that any fool could have laughed at, but there was also a sincerity, a kind of shining integrity, that made me turn again to the frontispiece and ponder over the dour sensitive face above the absurd dickey and the ill-fitting clothes. "Starcleuch Edge", by John Caverton. . . Starcleuch Edge . . . I began to remember . . .

About half-way through the war, I had transferred to a mountain-warfare unit, and our training took us out on rough country in all weathers. One day, we were on a scheme, deep in the Border hills, and a section of us had to hold a hill-top with a Bren-post, against all comers. The name of the hill was Starcleuch Edge. Remembering it now, as the train jogged along, I couldn't blame old Caverton for writing about it – a sombre heavy-shouldered Atlas of a hill whose dark jut of peak made it a landmark for half the Border.

When we had reached this peak, the staff-sergeant in charge of us, a professional, who would have considered Pisgah only for its field of fire, said, "Right, me lucky lads. This top' no good. No cover. But there's a dip on the uvver side, see? Just the job, only needs a little parapet. What d'you call these 'ere' eaps o' road-metal on Scotch 'ills, Jock?"

"Cairns, sarge?" I said,

"Right. Demolish cairn. It's 'alf fallen down already. Roll boulders dahn to reinforce fire-position. You, you, and you, for the bowling-alley. Remainder at the receiving end. And quick, me lads, afore the mad major storms the 'eights of Abraham with the 'ole ruddy battalion!"

Now apart from destroying the cairn, which I hadn't liked doing, there was something else that had bothered me then, and it began to bother me again, as I remembered the incident. It was the essential wrongness of rolling the stones. I could see them bouncing and trundling down the steep slope. But why not? Because . . .because . . . because . . .cairn stones are usually flat slabs. And cairns are built in the same way as dry-stone dykes. These stones had been rounded. They had come from a river or a burn. There were no dykes on Starcleuch Edge – as the sergeant had noted with blasphemous relish, for the major loved dry-stone dykes and their cover. The hill was a volcanic stump, and material for a cairn simply wasn't available. Why had someone raided the bed of a burn to build one? I had no answer. But the day was my own. I decided to get off the train a couple of stations sooner than I had intended. I wanted to find out about the cairn – and about John Caverton who had so fiercely praised the hill it had been built on.

Mr William Sudden of the "Border Sentinel" received me very affably. I laid the shabby little book before him, and asked for information.

"John Caverton", he mused, scratching his shock of white hair. "John Caverton". Man, it's a long time since I heard that name. But I remember him. And the printing of this wee book. He must have asked my father about the cost of printing it, long before my time. And I think he would scrimp and save for years to raise the money. For when I was a laddie of – oh, about sixteen, he came tramping into this office one day, in his great tacketty boots. He was a shepherd, a queer dour chap. And he fished a bundle of manuscript out of his maud-neuk . . ."

"Maud-neuk?"

"Aye. The pocket of his plaid. Then he counted down a pile of sovereigns, and told my father to get on with the printing."

"How many copies?"

"Oh, I think it was two hundred. But they never sold. They lay about here for years. Matter of fact, I gave them away for paper salvage during the war. About a hundred and fifty of them."

"Poor devil," I said.

"Aye, maybe. But he was ambitious, mind you. He sent away ten or a dozen review copies. But only one paper of any standing gave him a notice. Better if they hadn't. Some clever young chiel tore them to bits – laughed at them. Caverton never got over that. He began to drink, hard. Then he did a spell in prison for assault".

"Assault?"

"Well, you know what people are. Someone with a drink or two in him and said "Aye, man. Some folk think they can write poetry, and others think different, eh?" And Caverton went for him. Cut him to pieces. He got six months. It was after he came out that he began building his cairn".

"Cairn?" I said. But I could guess where.

"Aye. A cairn on the top of Starcleuch Edge. It was out on the far side of the hirsel. He must have carried a stone from the burn every time he looked his sheep. Nobody knew why. He was just written off as daft. But it all came out when he died."

"When was that?"

"Oh, let's see, now. About . . . 1903 . . . or 4. Here's the file . .April . .May . . That's lucky! June, 1904 . . . John Caverton . . .Cottage Hospital . . . aged fifty. Not an old man . . ."

"then . . then this is his centenary year".

"Aye, now. So it is. Well, well."

"You said something came out after his death? About the cairn."

"Aye." The old man chuckled. "He left a will. And twenty pounds. The will said it was to pay for his burial beside his cairn. But the whole thing was a farce."

"What kind of farce?"

"Well, the top of Starcleuch Edge is solid rock. He should have known that himself. You couldn't go down two feet without striking the foundations of Scotland. And to crown all, his widow turned up to claim the money. She had run off, years before, with an Irish roadman. A wild slattern of a creature. There were no children. So Caverton got a cheap funeral, and she boozed what was left with her man, and disappeared."

I thanked him, and rose to go.

"By the way," he said, "it wouldn't be worth your while looking for his grave in the cemetery. It was unmarked. There was some talk of putting a wee stone up by public subscription at the time. But it fell through. Aye. His jail record, you know . . .Aye."

"I've been thinking," I said. "It's quite usual to re-value writers round about their centenaries. I would be very pleased to do you a half-column on John Caverton – without payment, of course. I think he deserved it."

He thought this over. "Well," he said, "we have two flower-shows and an agricultural show, this week. And the football's started again. And we have a half-page advertisement from a multiple tailor to fit in as well . . ."

I could see that a bardie who had been born a hundred years ago was no use to him. "Alright", I said. "When can I get a bus to the water-head?"

He looked at his watch. "There's one in ten minutes from the market-place."

An hour later, I was well up on the shoulder of Starcleuch Edge, and wondering where the other half of my wind had gone to, in the last ten years. I was also beginning to wonder what exactly I hoped to achieve up there. But I kept steadily on, just the same. The going was heavy, and the hills were brindled tawny and plush green in the fitful blinks of sunshine, with a racing, ragged sky overhead. Wisps of rain-cloud were tearing along the heights, and my own objective was deep in driving mist at the summit. After a long pull I reached the old gun-post – a tumble of stones, now. A green-crusted cartridge-case clinked against my boot as I humped past. But we had held the position. The major had been cross. Very cross indeed.

As I struggled up the last steep rise to the peak, I could see something white gleaming through the mist. Something white . . . that resolved itself when I stood panting beside it, into a four-foot high squared cone of concrete with a flat top. It was brand new, and firmly based on the spot the cairn had occupied, and it looked good and solid enough to last for centuries.

There was a metal plate let into the top, with the words "Triangulation Station" deeply cut into it. Far more deeply cut and permanent than the words I scratched on the side with my pocket-knife in the driving mist and the crying of the wind: "John Caverton – Makar – 1854-1904". I didn't make a very good job, and I could only hope that her Majesty's Ordnance Survey wouldn't' mind.

THE CHILDREN

THE CHILDREN

Our children, we think,
Will always stay.
We love them so:
They will not go away,

Will always stay
To hear stories and play,
Old catches and snatches
To sing and to say.

We give to our own
What we learned in our day,
To the dearly loved
To take away.

1977

GLOSSARY

A

aith	oath
arles	payment
auld-farrant	old-fashioned, antiquated

B

benty	coarse, wiry
biggin	building
biggit	built
blashes	heavy falls
bruckle	frail, weak
bruisslt	sweating

C

churlin	making slight sounds
cleeds	clothes
craik	croak
croochin	huddling up
crup thegither	shrunk
curran	currant

D

Demeter	goddess of the harvest
dottle	plug of tobacco left in a pipe

E

emmet	ant
elleree	a person of preternatural insight

F

Fient anither	not another
Fraximus Excelsior	ash tree
forfochen	exhausted
Fraith	foam

G

gledge	squint, glance
gledgin	glancing
gleg	quick
glisk	glimpse
graith	clothing
grosert	gooseberry
gumpit	guddled

H

hauf-sweir	reluctant
hullerie	with feathers erect

J

Jooral-I-Joo	One Man Band
Jougals	dogs

K

kimmers	gossips
kay	key

L

Lacrimae Rerum	Tears of Things (Lat.)
lirk	crease, wrinkle, fold
luif	hand

M

murnin	lamenting
maa	seagull

P

pretensic	pretentious
paiks	blows, beatings

R

relict	remains of a dead person
rax	strain

S

scowderdowp	blacksmith (col.)
scurryvaig	a ragged vagrant
sennicht	a week ago
shilpit	thin
shootin-cheese	a cheese presented to the gossips by the father, when a child is born
shundert	covered in cinders
shuttle-gobbit	having a misshapen mouth
skaith	injury, damage (also scaith)
smarroch	crowd, collection
snirkin	sniggering
souch	sigh
sough	frenzy
spaik	roosting bar
speiled	climbed
spreit	spirit
steeks	stitches
stravaigin	wandering aimlessly

T

thole his assize	undergo his trial
tod	fox
tossilit	tassled
trock(ed)	dealing/dealt

W

wae	sorrowful
wairpit	warped
wames	stomachs
warstle	wrestle
weel-faured	attractive
whalp	puppy
whuds	lies
whustlecrowdie	a composition of oatmeal, boiled water and butter
wight	brave
wirriecow	bugbear
wyle	deceive
wyte	blame, responsibility

Y

yammerin	groaning
yits	oats